THE ALTAR
and the
ALTARPIECE

THE ALTAR
and the
ALTARPIECE

Sacramental Themes
in Early Netherlandish Painting

BARBARA G. LANE

ICON EDITIONS

1817

HARPER & ROW, PUBLISHERS, New York

Cambridge, Philadelphia, San Francisco, London
Mexico City, São Paulo, Sydney

To J.M.L., D.A.L., and J.T.L.

FIRST EDITION

Designer: C. Linda Dingler

Library of Congress Cataloging in Publication Data

Lane, Barbara G.
    The altar and the altarpiece.

    (Icon editions)
    Bibliography: p.
    1. Altarpieces, Flemish. 2. Altarpieces, Gothic
—Belgium. 3. Altarpieces, Dutch. 4. Altarpieces,
Gothic—Netherlands. 5. Mass in art. 6. Christian
art and symbolism—Medieval, 500-1500. I. Title.
ND635.L36 1984   755'.2'09492   83-48364
ISBN 0-06-435000-2   84 85 86 87 88 89 10 9 8 7 6 5 4 3 2 1
ISBN 0-06-430133-8 (pbk.)   84 85 86 87 88 89 10 9 8 7 6 5 4 3 2 1

Contents

Acknowledgments

This study owes its inspiration to the constant stimulation and profound insights of Professor Lotte Brand Philip. Her unfailing support and constructive criticism contributed in invaluable and innumerable ways to its completion.

The photographs reproduced here were purchased with the aid of a Rutgers University Research Council Faculty Fellowship. I am especially grateful to the staffs of the Pierpont Morgan Library, the Index of Christian Art in Princeton, and the Library of the Union Theological Seminary for providing me with unlimited access to their collections. Dr. Jacqueline Folie and the generous staff at the Institut Royal du Patrimoine Artistique in Brussels assisted me in obtaining obscure information and photographs, and Professor Myra Uhlfelder kindly offered her valuable opinions on the Latin translations. I would also like to thank Professors Walter Gibson and Robert Koch for their perceptive readings of an earlier version of the text.

Of the many individuals involved in transforming the final manuscript into book form, certain members of the Harper & Row staff deserve special mention: Bitite Vinklers, for her meticulous copy editing; C. Linda Dingler, for her creative design; Edmée Reit, for her tireless work on the index; and Pamela Jelley, for her dependable calm in many a frantic moment. Above all, I am grateful to Cass Canfield, Jr., for his initial confidence in this project, his valuable suggestions concerning revisions, and his maintenance of the highest standards in every stage of production.

THE ALTAR
and the
ALTARPIECE

1. Robert Campin, *Madonna and Child Before a Fire Screen,* 25 x 19¼″ (63.5 x 49 cm).
London, The National Gallery.

Introduction

The service of the altar is the nucleus of the Church's worship, just as the altar-table is the central point of the church building. Therefore, church art ought also, it would seem, to be explicable in its character and purpose, if considered in connection with the ritual performed at the altar.[1]

—*Yrjö Hirn*, The Sacred Shrine

The intimate connection between religious art and the liturgical ceremonies it illustrates ought to be self-evident. In the late Middle Ages, it certainly needed no explanation for the generations of worshipers who saw paintings over the altar every day when they attended Mass. Today, however, altarpieces all too frequently adorn museum walls instead of altars. The modern viewer often responds more to their style and technique than to the theological messages they were intended to convey. In a period when we must strain our imagination to comprehend the religious fervor of earlier eras, it is difficult to remember that these paintings were created to fulfill basic ecclesiastical needs.

Nowhere is this problem more crucial than in the field of fifteenth-century painting in the Netherlands. Students are initially attracted to works of this period by their brilliance of color and fascination with detail, but soon they begin to complain that the subjects are "too religious." Museum visitors, captivated by the jewel-like radiance of the enchanting panels they see in the galleries, express wonder at the infrequency of secular themes.

This study attempts to lead the reader from the skeptical world of the twentieth century into an age of overwhelming piety, when paintings were ecclesiastical objects that explained the rituals celebrated at the altars they adorned. Instead of approaching early Netherlandish painting

1

from the traditional viewpoint of stylistic development, it concentrates on the major religious themes of the period. Its aim is to contribute to an understanding of how these exquisite altarpieces dramatized the meaning of the Mass for the worshiper.

No period of art surpasses early Netherlandish painting in the combination of convincing visual reality and overwhelming spiritual intensity. With their unprecedented development of the oil medium and their new interest in the depiction of believable space, the painters from Robert Campin to Memling were able to bring the miracles of church doctrine to life more concretely and vividly than any previous artists. They portrayed traditional subjects in realistic settings that created a new intimacy for the worshiper. Yet they also managed to instill these scenes with profound theological meanings that eloquently dramatized the church rituals. Every altarpiece necessarily relates to the altar beneath it. Early Netherlandish altarpieces, however, evoke the ceremonies performed at the altar with unparalleled originality, subtlety, and fervor.

One example by Robert Campin will illustrate the extraordinary reinterpretation of traditional themes that characterizes early Netherlandish paintings. The *Madonna and Child Before a Fire Screen* in London (Fig. 1)[2] depicts the seated Virgin in a room filled with domestic objects. Behind her, a long bench partially covers a circular fire screen that all but obscures a blazing fire. An open book rests on this bench, and a three-legged stool stands to the left of it. In the upper left corner, folding shutters open to reveal a view of a fifteenth-century Flemish town through the window. Only the chalice that rests on an ornately carved cabinet at the right seems out of place in this humble, everyday setting.

In the midst of this deceptively simple interior, Mary holds the Christ Child gently with her left arm as she apparently prepares her right breast to nurse him. Her position close to the ground has led scholars to describe her as a "Madonna of Humility."[3] As Davies has observed,[4] however, the numerous genre elements in Campin's painting are unprecedented in pictures of this subject.[5]

The theme of the Madonna of Humility seems to have originated in Trecento Italian painting.[6] It was still popular in the middle of the fifteenth century, as, for example, in Giovanni di Paolo's large panel of about 1455–60 in New York (Fig. 2).[7] This picture postdates Campin's panel by at least thirty years, and yet it reveals no desire to create a realistic space. It depicts an elaborately garbed, graceful Madonna against a patternized background, as in so many earlier Italian interpretations of the

2. Giovanni di Paolo, *Madonna and Child with Angels,* 54½ x 32″ (137.8 x 81.3 cm). New York, Metropolitan Museum of Art, Bequest of George Blumenthal, 1941.

theme. Two angels, on either side of the Virgin, contribute to the removal of this image from the earthly world of the observer. The large, flat halos of the holy figures emphasize their sanctity. Only the kneeling supplicant in the lower left corner suggests that a worshiper might enter this scene, but his diminutive scale immediately differentiates him from the enormous Virgin.

Although Giovanni di Paolo's Madonna sits on the ground, she clearly inhabits a spiritual realm. In contrast, Campin's Virgin occupies a room in a simple Flemish house. This humble scene presents the viewer with a tantalizing paradox. Why should the timeless image of the Virgin and Child include a fifteenth-century domestic interior? How can Mary display the body of Christ in a space that is anything but sacramental? No text justifies the placement of these holy figures in such a common setting. Many details of this room suggest, in fact, that it is less "domestic" than it first appears.

Scholars have often recognized that Campin's circular fire screen acts as a halo around Mary's head.[8] A flat, gold halo like the one in the Italian panel would not have met the demands of the new realistic style. Campin's ingenious placement of the fire screen behind the Madonna simultaneously retains the symbolic meaning of a halo and contributes to the realism of the setting.

The liturgical chalice on the table at the extreme right seems too elegant for its humble surroundings. Since it occurs in a restored strip at the right side of the panel, some writers consider it a modern addition.[9] It is possible, however, that the restoration is close to the appearance of the original missing section, as Panofsky has suggested.[10] The inclusion of a liturgical chalice in this composition is, in fact, perfectly logical. As the container of the sacramental wine during Mass, it refers to Christ's blood. Similarly, the Christ Child on the Virgin's lap is a visual explanation of the meaning of the consecrated Host. Together, the chalice and the Child, placed close to each other on the same level in the picture, refer to the substance of the Eucharist.

O'Meara has recently explained the fireplace behind the Virgin in relation to the analogy between bread baked on the hearth and the Infant Christ, the "living bread," who was formed in Mary's womb. She recognized that the fire refers to the Old Testament burnt offerings that prefigure the sacrifice of the New Law, Christ. In Campin's painting, the Virgin encases the Child with her body as the fireplace contains the fire; as the bearer of the "living bread," she is the New Testament replacement for the hearth of the Old Law.[11]

3. *Virgin and Child, Très Belles Heures de Jean de Berry,*
c. 10⅞ x 7¼″ (c. 27.5 x 18.5 cm). Brussels, Bibliothèque
Royale.

The fire screen, the chalice, and the fireplace contribute to the identification of this apparently domestic setting as the sacred abode of the
body of Christ. The inclusion of these symbolic objects is, however, only
part of the revolutionary change that has occurred in Campin's panel. His
scene also differs from the Italian version in the positions of the Madonna
and Child.

Giovanni di Paolo's Virgin holds the Christ Child in her lap with both
hands. As the Infant nurses in this painting, he grasps Mary's breast and
looks at the viewer out of the corners of his eyes. This posture also occurs
in early northern interpretations of the theme, such as the dedication

4. *Virgin and Child, Heures de Milan*, 11⅛ x 8⅛" (28.4 x 20.5 cm). Turin, Museo Civico.

miniature of about 1390 in the *Très Belles Heures de Jean de Berry* in Brussels (Fig. 3).[12] Although Campin may have known such images, he did not echo the positions of their figures. In his painting, Christ does not nurse. He turns his whole body outward in order to gaze at us more easily, and, perhaps, in order to invite our participation. Mary gently touches her breast with her right hand and directs it away from the Infant toward the viewer himself.[13]

Comparison of this image with earlier scenes of the lactating Virgin clarifies its meaning. In a miniature of about 1380–85 from the Milan section of the "Turin-Milan Hours" (Fig. 4),[14] for instance, Mary glances toward a kneeling supplicant as she presses milk from her breast. Here, again, the Infant makes no attempt to nurse, and it is clear that the milk is intended for the benefit of the worshiper.

The nursing Madonna is an intercessory image.[15] In late medieval thought, Mary's pleas for the salvation of mankind were granted by virtue of the breasts with which she nursed Christ. As I have discussed elsewhere,[16] images of the Virgin presenting her breast often accompanied figures of Christ exposing his wounds to God the Father to form the so-called "Double Intercession": for example, in a later miniature from the "Turin-Milan Hours" that probably dates in the middle of the fifteenth century (Fig. 5).[17] In each of these scenes, Mary touches her breast, which

5. *Christ and the Virgin Interceding with God the Father,* "Turin-Milan Hours," 11⅛ x 8⅛" (28.4 x 20.5 cm). Paris, Musée du Louvre, Cabinet des Dessins.

she does not normally do in a portrayal of the Madonna of Humility. When she holds the Child on her lap and presents her breast to a worshiper, as in Figure 4, it is her intercessory role that is emphasized. This particular miniature, in fact, illustrates the Saturday Mass of the Virgin, in which Mary's intercession is the major theme.[18]

Whereas Campin must have known the Italian tradition of the nursing Madonna of Humility, either from direct contact with Trecento panels or from northern interpretations of them, his painting explicitly concentrates on the intercessory implications of the theme. Mary's gesture forces the viewer to focus on the object that enables her to act on his behalf. We know, moreover, that the Infant originally looked toward the Virgin's breast.[19] The deliberate change in the direction of his glance illustrates Campin's desire to convey the idea that Mary offers her gift to the viewer himself.

Campin's painting differs from the traditional Madonna of Humility in its substitution of a realistic interior space for a gold or patternized background. The new setting, however, is still sacred, as its symbolic objects indicate. It acts as a shrine that encases the body of Christ and as the sanctuary where the Transubstantiation, the miraculous transformation of the bread and wine into the body and blood of Christ, occurs. It presents Mary as the bearer of the New Testament sacrifice and as the primary intercessor for mankind.

We have no information about the original function of Campin's panel. It may have served as an object for private contemplation and devotion. Its emphasis on Mary's intercession, however, would have made it equally suitable for use during the service devoted specifically to that subject, the Saturday Mass of the Virgin. Since this panel clearly illustrates the meaning of the Eucharistic bread and wine, however, it is also an eloquent explanation of the daily sacrifice of Mass. It is, therefore, perfectly logical as an altarpiece in a church or private chapel where Mass was celebrated.

The vivid, dramatic explanation of the Mass that appears in this panel recurs throughout fifteenth-century Netherlandish painting and differentiates the works of this period from earlier altar paintings.[20] As in countless examples of church decoration throughout the Middle Ages, in fresco and stained glass as well as panel painting, these altarpieces had to illustrate the meaning of the daily liturgical ceremonies for the congregation. Unlike the earlier works, however, they portray timeless theological truths in terms of the worshiper's own everyday experience.

In order to comprehend the complex meanings of early Netherlandish altarpieces, we must approach them as ecclesiastical objects. We must try to understand why certain devotional themes recur so often throughout the fifteenth century. Although only a fraction of the original number of panels that were produced in the period remains, the prevalence of a few specific subjects in the extant works suggests their widespread popularity. The most common themes are deliberately ritualistic rather than anecdotal, in spite of their frequent emphasis on specific details of everyday reality. Throughout the century, the preserved "narratives" concentrate almost exclusively on Christ's Infancy and Passion. His ministry and appearances after the Resurrection occur with astonishing infrequency. Although examples of these subjects may be lost to us today, it can hardly be coincidental that the recurrent scenes of Christ's birth and sacrifice in early Netherlandish painting depict the most basic themes of the Catholic liturgy.

The sparse documentation preserved for this period does not, unfortunately, always permit us to be certain about the original locations of the paintings. Whereas some of these works certainly adorned high altars, others probably decorated smaller altars in side chapels. Some of the smaller panels were used in private, domestic worship or as doors covering a Host recess below a large altarpiece.[21] No matter where they were located, however, these radiant panels had to explain the meaning of the church ceremonies they were commissioned to illustrate.

Traditional studies of early Netherlandish painting have concentrated on stylistic development and iconographic analysis rather than on the problem of how these works functioned in their own period. Recent scholars such as Philip and Blum, however, have investigated the relationships of some of these paintings to their intended settings.[22] Benjamin has departed from earlier approaches by searching for a reason for the sudden development of the new realistic style. He has proposed that the believable settings depicted in these works resulted from the requirements of the *Devotio Moderna,* the Netherlandish religious movement in which the strong emphasis on devout meditation encouraged intimacy in the portrayal of sacred subjects.[23]

As Benjamin has suggested, the enhancement of the worshiper's devotional experience must have been one of the aims of the new realistic settings that appear in the works of this period. As statements of timeless theological truths, these paintings are similar to the traditional "Andachtsbilder" used so frequently for private meditation.[24] Their timelessness, however, made them equally suitable as illustrations of the daily church rituals that constantly repeated the sacrifice of Christ.

It is the liturgical function of these intimate works that is the focus here. This study introduces the reader to the major sacramental themes in early Netherlandish painting and reviews the essential considerations of these themes in recent literature. It includes restatements of some of my earlier investigations in the context of the entire period, as well as extensive discussion and documentation of previously unpublished material. Its aim is to concentrate on selected examples that illustrate most clearly the intimate relationship between these dazzling paintings and the ceremonies that they dramatized.

NOTES TO INTRODUCTION

1. Hirn, 73.

2. National Gallery. For this painting, also known as the "Salting Madonna" and usually considered an early work of c. 1420–25 by Campin, see especially Friedländer, II, #58; Panofsky, 163f.; Davies, *National Gallery,* 65ff.; Davies, *Early Netherlandish School,* 25ff.; and Davies, 253. Throughout this study, Robert Campin is accepted as the "Master of Flémalle." For the controversy concerning the Flémalle works, see the remarks below in the Brief Biographies of Early Netherlandish Artists.

3. E.g., Meiss ("Madonna of Humility," 451, and *Painting in Florence and Siena,* 143 and 156) and Panofsky, 163.

4. Davies, 253; cf. his remarks in *National Gallery,* 66, and *Early Netherlandish School,* 26.

5. For Italian examples of the "domestic type" of this theme, which include only minimal suggestions of interiors, see the sources cited in the following note.

6. See Meiss, "Madonna of Humility," 436ff., and *Painting in Florence and Siena,* 145ff. for arguments concerning the Sienese origin of the theme.

7. Metropolitan Museum of Art. For this painting, see F. Zeri and E. E. Gardner, *Italian Paintings. A Catalogue of the Collection of the Metropolitan Museum of Art. Sienese*

and Central Italian Schools, New York, 1980, 28f. and pl. 46.

8. E.g., Panofsky, 163; Davies, 253; and, most recently, Purtle, 100.

9. E.g., Friedländer, II, 71. This was first proposed by J. Destrée, "Altered in the Nineteenth Century? A Problem at the National Gallery, London," *Connoisseur,* LXXIV, 1926, 209f.

10. Panofsky, 164.

11. For this interpretation, see O'Meara, 82f.

12. Brussels, Bibliothèque Royale, ms. 11060–61, p. 11. For this manuscript and the controversy over the authorship of this miniature, see especially Meiss, 198ff. and 321ff.

13. This has been noted by O'Meara, 82.

14. This part of the frequently divided "Turin-Milan Hours" is preserved as the *Heures de Milan* in the Museo Civico in Turin. For the history of this section of the manuscript, see Meiss, 107ff. and 337ff.; Meiss attributes this miniature (fol. 120) to the Master of the Parement de Narbonne and his workshop.

15. For the intercessory character of this theme, see especially Meiss, "Madonna of Humility," 460f., and *Painting in Florence and Siena,* 151f.

16. Lane, "Symbolic Crucifixion," 10ff.

17. Paris, Musée du Louvre, Cabinet des

Dessins, RF 2025. For this miniature, see *ibid.,* 19f., with further literature cited in nn. 77–81. A good review of the problem of the dating of the unfinished section of this manuscript appears in J. Marrow's review of P. Durrieu, *Heures de Turin,* reprint by A. Châtelet of the 1902 edition, Turin, 1967, in *Art Bulletin,* L, 1968, 203ff.

18. For a discussion of this theme in the Saturday Mass and the visual tradition connected with it, see Lane, "Symbolic Crucifixion," 6ff.

19. See, e.g., Davies, 253.

20. Cf. the eloquent discussion of this contrast in Philip, 165ff.

21. For an example of this latter type, see below, Ch. IV, pp. 128–130.

22. Whereas Philip has concentrated on a single work, the Ghent Altarpiece (Philip), Blum has studied eleven separate triptychs (Blum).

23. Benjamin, 11ff. For the *Devotio Moderna,* see especially R. R. Post, *The Modern Devotion: Confrontation with Reformation and Humanism,* Leyden, 1968.

24. For the problem of the definition of the term "Andachtsbild," see especially Ringbom, 55ff.

I
Altar and Tabernacle

The altar has always occupied the place of honor in the Catholic church. In the Middle Ages, it was the center of the action in performances of liturgical dramas written for special feast days, as well as during the celebration of Mass itself. It was here that the celebrant offered the Eucharistic sacrifice that was the dramatic climax of the daily ritual. During Mass, the altar was the resting place of the consecrated wafer of the Host. A gold plate, known as a paten, held this wafer above the white cloth, or corporal, that covered the altar. After Mass, the Host was often displayed on the altar in a container made especially for that purpose. The altar was, therefore, the primary place for the support and display of the bread that had been transformed into the body of Christ.[1]

Whereas the altar surpassed all other liturgical furnishings in its essential use during Mass, a second object was just as intimately connected with the Eucharistic wafer: the tabernacle. From the earliest Christian times, consecrated wafers that were to be used after Mass were reserved in containers placed on or near the altar. Although many different names have been invented to classify the various shapes of these containers, the term "tabernacle" can be applied to all of them.[2] They all were created for a single, sacred purpose: to conserve and protect the consecrated Host.

Early Netherlandish painters alluded to the altar and the tabernacle in images of the major intercessor for man's salvation, the Virgin Mary. The aim of this chapter is to explain how and why they compared the Madonna with these liturgical objects.

Representations of the Virgin and Child appear more frequently in early Netherlandish painting than any other subject. The artists of these panels drew their inspiration from a multitude of earlier images of Mary,

6. Jan van Eyck, Lucca *Madonna*, 25¾ x 19½″ (65.5 x 49.5 cm). Frankfurt, Städelsches Kunstinstitut.

whose popularity climaxed in the Gothic period. They certainly did not invent the complex web of meaning that they wove around the Madonna; rather, they expressed her traditional symbols in new, realistic terms.[3] This chapter does not attempt to survey all of the symbolism in these complex pictures. Instead, it concentrates on the Eucharistic implications of the settings in a few selected examples.

Jan van Eyck's Lucca Madonna

In his Lucca *Madonna* of about 1436, in Frankfurt (Fig. 6),[4] Jan van Eyck portrayed a statuesque Virgin on an elaborate canopied throne, in a narrow, box-like space that defies precise analysis. As a throne room, this interior is unusual for its lack of any regal associations other than the throne itself. Yet the ordinary objects in the niche at the right hardly suffice to identify it as a domestic setting. The action of the figures is no less problematic, for the rigidly erect posture of the Christ Child is certainly not the natural pose of a nursing infant. In spite of Jan's phenomenal attention to realistic detail, the scene is strangely removed from the everyday world.

Scholars have frequently identified the theme of the Throne of Solo-

7. *The Throne of Wisdom*, 43¼ x 81⅞″ (110 x 208 cm). Berlin, Staatliche Museen Preussischer Kulturbesitz, Gemäldegalerie.

8. *Enthroned Virgin as the Throne of Wisdom*, 54¼ x 24"(138 x 56 cm). Liège, St. Jean.

mon in this curiously remote picture.[5] The four lions that adorn Mary's throne allude to the twelve lions on the sides and steps of Solomon's majestic throne (1 Kings 10:18–20 and 2 Chronicles 9:17–19). The *Speculum Humanae Salvationis* of the fourteenth century explains the parallel as follows: "The throne of the true Solomon is the most Blessed Virgin Mary,/ In which sat Jesus Christ, the true Wisdom."[6] Writers have devoted so much attention to this symbolism in recent years that its popularity in medieval art and thought need not detain us here.[7] Jan did not include the twelve lions that appear in Gothic painted versions of the theme, such as a fourteenth-century Westphalian panel in Berlin (Fig. 7).[8] The Lucca *Madonna* is, in fact, closer to earlier carved precedents. Jan's volumetric Virgin recalls such elegant, solemn statues of the Throne of Wisdom as the Mosan example of the middle of the thirteenth century in Liège (Fig. 8).[9] Although no lions appear in these carved Madonnas, Mary's rectilinear body always serves as Christ's throne in them, as it does in Jan's painting.

9. Jan van Eyck, Dresden Triptych, 10⅞ x 14¾″ (27.5 x 37.5 cm). Dresden, Staatliche Kunstammlungen, Gemäldegalerie Alte Meister.

The Throne of Wisdom is certainly not the only major theme in the Lucca *Madonna.* Its nursing Virgin refers to Mary's intercession, as in the examples mentioned in the Introduction. This idea is less pronounced than in Campin's *Madonna and Child Before a Fire Screen* (Fig. 1), however, since neither Mary nor the Christ Child invites the viewer's participation. The remoteness of these figures in Jan's painting results, in fact, from their Eucharistic associations.

In the Lucca *Madonna,* Mary's rigidly horizontal lap resembles the flat surface of a table. On it, she holds the nursing infant stiffly, on a white piece of cloth. The Christ Child sits on Mary's shelf-like lap as the wafer of the Host rests on the white corporal, on the altar, during Mass. Jan has interpreted the Virgin as the altar of Christ.[10]

The niche to the right of the Virgin's throne contributes to this identification. Its top shelf contains a glass vial of water and a candlestick, both traditional symbols of the Virgin.[11] The basin of water below these objects, however, has a liturgical function.[12] Throughout the Middle Ages, it was customary for the priest to wash his hands before and after Mass at a niche, or *piscina,* that was usually located on the south side of the altar.[13] Such niches contained lavers and basins or drains provided for this purpose.[14] Whereas the basin seems out of place in a throne room, it is completely logical in a sanctuary, beside the living counterpart of the altar.

Scholars have occasionally described Mary as the altar in the Eyckian panels that portray the most clearly ecclesiastical settings. In the Dresden Triptych (Fig. 9), for instance, Jan depicted the enthroned Virgin in the central panel at the end of a long nave, whose columns clearly separate it from the aisles that continue the space in the wings of the altarpiece. Since Mary appears here in the apse of a basilica, where one would expect to find an altar, she seems to replace the altar itself.[15] Whether the interior of the *Madonna of Canon van der Paele* in Bruges (Fig. 10) depicts an apse or a centrally planned church, it also portrays Mary in the place of honor that is usually reserved for the high altar. The canon kneels before her as he would kneel in prayer before an altar at Mass.[16] Countless earlier devotional images include worshipers praying at the altar in exactly this manner: for example, a late-fourteenth-century miniature in the *Petites Heures du Duc de Berry* in Paris (Fig. 70).[17] In both the Dresden Triptych

10. Jan van Eyck, *Madonna of Canon van der Paele,* 48⅛ x 62⅛″ (122.1 x 157.8 cm). Bruges, Groeninge Museum.

11. Jan van Eyck, *Madonna of Chancellor Rolin,* 26 x 24⅜″ (66 x 62 cm). Paris, Musée du Louvre.

and the *Madonna of Canon van der Paele,* the Christ Child sits on a white cloth on the flat lap of the Virgin, whose form echoes the rectilinearity of the throne itself.

Mary's statuesque body replaces the throne entirely in a third example, the *Madonna of Chancellor Rolin* in Paris (Fig. 11), where she again holds the rigid body of Christ on her shelf-like lap.[18] Van Buren has recently suggested that this painting hung on the east wall of Rolin's chapel in Autun, to the left of the actual altar.[19] In this location, Mary would have appeared between Rolin and the altar that he faced, as a dramatic visual parallel of the table that supported the Eucharistic wafer.

12. Rogier van der Weyden, Bladelin Triptych, left wing:
Augustus and the Tiburtine Sibyl, 35⅞ x 15¾″ (91 x 40 cm).
Berlin, Staatliche Museen Preussischer Kulturbesitz,
Gemäldegalerie.

13. Rogier van der Weyden, Bladelin Triptych, left wing,
detail: Mary as the *Ara Coeli.*

Scholars have explained Jan's explicit interpretation of the Virgin as
the altar in relationship to the legend of the *Ara Coeli.*[20] According to this
legend, Emperor Augustus asked the Tiburtine Sibyl if there would ever
be a man greater than he. In response, she revealed a vision of the Virgin

and Child on the day of Christ's birth. At the moment of the vision, a voice proclaimed, "This woman is the Altar of Heaven" *(Ara Coeli)*. Although this story originated in the sixth century,[21] it was popularized by the thirteenth-century compilation of legends by Jacobus da Voragine, the widely read *Legenda Aurea,* as well as the later *Speculum Humanae Salvationis.*[22]

The legend of the *Ara Coeli* appears in only one major early Netherlandish painting: the left wing of Rogier van der Weyden's Bladelin Triptych in Berlin (Fig. 12).[23] In this panel, Augustus looks through an opened window at the glowing vision of the Virgin, who sits upright on an actual altar and holds the Child in the center of her lap (Fig. 13). It may not be coincidental that Rogier's "Altar of Heaven" is more rigid and less tender than his other images of Mary (cf. Figs. 16 and 19). The angularity of her body recalls all of Jan's enthroned Virgins. Her pose, in fact, is strangely reminiscent of the Rolin *Madonna* (Fig. 11). It is possible that Rogier's statuesque figure of the *Ara Coeli* in this panel deliberately echoes Jan's analogy between the Virgin and the altar.

The legend of Augustus and the Tiburtine Sibyl does not explain *why* Mary is called the Altar of Heaven. Other sources for this idea, however, are more specific. Byzantine writers, for instance, praised the Virgin as the living altar of the bread of life.[24] As the bearer of Christ, she was compared to the altar that carries the Eucharist. Mary's offering of her son was equated with the oblation, or daily sacrifice, of Mass, since both occur for the salvation of mankind.[25] In the west, *mensa,* the common Latin name for altar, was one of her many epithets.[26]

The most elaborate explanations of the idea of Mary as the altar of the bread of life, the *mensa panis vitae,* occur, however, in sources that compare her to the golden table of the Sun. This parallel appears in the *Speculum Humanae Salvationis,* in the chapter on the Presentation of the Virgin in the Temple.[27] Ludolphus of Saxony abbreviated the passage from the *Speculum* in his popular meditational treatise on Christ's life, the *Vita Christi* of about 1325.[28]

The legend of the *Mensa Solis in Sabulo* concerns a golden table that some fishermen discovered in the sea. Chapter V of the *Speculum* relates that the fishermen built a temple on the shore where they had found the table, and dedicated both the temple and the table to their god, the Sun. The passage equates the offering of the table with the presentation of the young Virgin in the temple, since both the golden table and Mary were made of the purest materials and were dedicated to the highest God. At

14. Petrus Christus, *Madonna with Saints Jerome and Francis,* 18⅛ x 17⅜″ (46 x 44 cm). Frankfurt, Städelsches Kunstinstitut.

this point in the narrative, however, the parallel suddenly shifts from the event in Mary's childhood to her offering of her son:

> Mary is well prefigured by the table of the sun,
> Because through her celestial food has been served to us;
> For she gave birth, for us, to the son of God, Jesus Christ,
> Who has revived us with his body and blood.
> Blessed be this most beautiful altar,
> Through whom food so healthful and so abundant has been
>   served to us! [29]

Ludolphus' brief summary of the legend culminates with an incomplete quotation from the *Speculum:* "And Mary is well prefigured by the table (*mensa*), because through her a celestial meal has been served to us." [30] His omission of *solis* ("of the sun") carries the analogy one step further away from the legend, in order to reinforce the parallel between Mary and the altar-table of Mass.

The inclusion of the Virgin-altar analogy in the *Speculum* and the *Vita Christi,* two of the most popular books of the late Middle Ages,[31] documents its prominence in fifteenth-century thought. Its transformation into statuesque images of the enthroned Madonna and Child is one of Jan van Eyck's most subtle and influential inventions. As we shall see in the next chapter, the portrayal of the Madonna as the altar recurred in countless panels through the century, in scenes of the Adoration of the Magi as well as the enthroned Virgin. Rarely, however, was this theme so effectively dramatized as in the Lucca *Madonna.*

Petrus Christus' Madonna with Saints Jerome and Francis

A fascinating adaptation of the Lucca *Madonna* hangs today in the same room of the Städelsches Kunstinstitut in Frankfurt: Petrus Christus' *Madonna with Saints* of 1457 (Fig. 14).[32] Here, the artist has moved the throne to a less confined setting, in which a window and door open onto a cheerful landscape. Saints Jerome and Francis flank the throne,[33] and the Christ Child sits in a more relaxed position. More significant than these changes, however, is the artist's elaboration of the Virgin-altar analogy.

In the Frankfurt *Madonna,* Christus added transparent columns to the Eyckian throne, as well as curtains that wind gracefully around them. If these curtains were loosened, they could be pulled around the sides and

15. *Madonna and Child,* 8⅝ x 3⅞″ (22 x 10 cm). Mainz, Mittelrheinisches Landesmuseum.

front of the Virgin's throne. Similarly, altar curtains were drawn around altars during the Transubstantiation, to hide the miracle from view and thereby enhance its mystery.[34] Hirn's comparison of Mary to the place of this ceremony is especially applicable to Christus' panel: ". . . her womb, that of a mother yet closed like a virgin's, is a magical room in the same way that the old altar-room enclosed with curtains was a sorcerer's cabinet, in which the great transformation took place without its process being visible."[35]

Christus' curtains may also have another meaning. Forsyth has suggested that the statues of the Throne of Wisdom (cf. Fig. 8) were placed on the altar during the *Officium Stellae,* the play of the Magi, which was performed at the Feast of the Epiphany.[36] Since stage directions for these plays often state that a curtain was withdrawn to reveal the Madonna and Child at the proper dramatic moment,[37] Forsyth has assumed that these statues were covered with baldachins hung with curtains.[38] Although no such baldachins survive to cover the preserved statues of the Throne of Wisdom, they do appear in many medieval reliefs of the Virgin and Child: for example, in an ivory of about 1010 in the Mittelrheinisches Landesmuseum in Mainz (Fig. 15).[39] Christus' addition of curtains suggests, therefore, that he understood the canopied thrones in Jan's panels as parallels to the baldachins that covered the carved Madonnas.

In Christus' painting, as in the numerous later Flemish panels that echo Jan's depiction of Mary as the altar,[40] the Christ Child on the Virgin's lap corresponds to the Host resting on the altar. The elaborate throne, with its decorative curtains, presents the worshiper with a visual parallel of the secret chamber where the priest enacted the miracle of Transubstantiation.

Rogier van der Weyden's *Thyssen* Madonna and Child

In contrast to the Lucca *Madonna* and the *Madonna with Saints* in Frankfurt, Rogier van der Weyden's exquisite little panel in the Thyssen Collection in Lugano (Fig. 16) places the Virgin and Child in the limited foreground space of a shallow niche. As in Jan's painting, however, the space must be symbolic, since the niche is too small for the size of the Virgin. Scholars usually interpret this niche as the portal of a Gothic church.[41] In his discussion of the symbolic space in pictures of Mary during this period, Panofsky called it "an outside chapel or oratory" that refers to Mary in the same way as the cathedral in Jan's Berlin *Madonna in a Church* ex-

16. Rogier van der Weyden, *Madonna and Child,* 5½ x 4⅛″ (14 x 10.5 cm). Lugano, Thyssen-Bornemisza Collection.

plains the meaning of the figure it encloses.[42] No one has explained, however, why this portal has no apparent relationship to the wall behind it. If this is a church portal, where is the church to which it is attached? Although this setting may characterize Mary as the Church, it probably also refers to her as the bearer of the incarnate Christ.

In order to understand the meaning of the limited space in the Thyssen *Madonna and Child,* one must define the traditional connection between the Virgin and a second ecclesiastical object that was intimately associated with the consecrated Host: the tabernacle. Since Mary's womb was the first receptacle of the body of Christ, she was naturally equated with the liturgical container that housed the Eucharistic wafers.[43]

The comparison of Mary with a tabernacle was especially popular in the twelfth century. Amadeus of Lausanne (d. 1159), for instance, declared, "Mary is a beautiful golden urn . . . this urn held the hidden manna, she who in her sacred womb bore the bread of the angels which comes down from heaven and gives life to the world."[44] Adam of St. Victor (d. before 1192) dramatized this idea in his famous hymn of Mary's birth:

> Hail mother of the saviour,
> chosen vessel, vessel of honor,
>   vessel of heavenly grace;
> Vessel foreseen from eternity,
> remarkable vessel, vessel forged
>   by the hand of wisdom.[45]

In his *Rationale Divinorum Officiorum* of the thirteenth century, William Durandus was even more specific: ". . . the box in which the consecrated Hosts are preserved signifies the body of the glorious Virgin."[46] The *Speculum Humanae Salvationis* (c. 1324) compares Mary to the ark of the Old Testament: "As the ark contained the golden urn with manna,/ So Mary offered us the true manna of heaven."[47] Innumerable hymns repeat this parallel in the late Gothic period.[48]

Before the fifteenth century, the most literal portrayals of the Virgin as a tabernacle occur in the so-called "Vierges ouvrantes."[49] In a German work of about 1300 at the Metropolitan Museum of Art in New York (Figs. 17 and 18), for instance, the two halves of Mary's body originally opened to reveal a carved image of the Trinity, of which only the figure of God the Father remains.[50] Flemish painters, however, found more realistic ways to convey the idea that the Virgin contained the body of Christ in her womb as the tabernacle houses the wafer of the Host.

17. *Vierge Ouvrante,* closed, 14½ x 5″ (36.8 x 12.7 cm). New York, Metropolitan Museum of Art, Gift of J. Pierpont Morgan, 1917.

18. *Vierge Ouvrante,* open, 14½ x 13⅝″ (36.8 x 34.6 cm). New York, Metropolitan Museum of Art, Gift of J. Pierpont Morgan, 1917.

19. Rogier van der Weyden, "Medici Madonna," 20⅞ x 15" (53 x 38 cm). Frankfurt,
Städelsches Kunstinstitut.

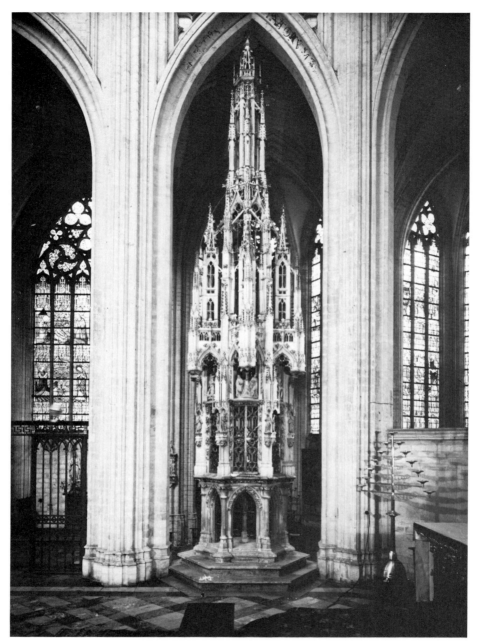

20. Sacrament House, height 41′ (12.05 m). Louvain, Collegiate Church of St. Peter.

21. Hans Memling, *Madonna and Child with Angels,* 23¼ x 18⅞″ (59 x 48 cm).
Washington, D.C., National Gallery of Art, Andrew Mellon Collection.

The most obvious expression of this theme in early Netherlandish painting occurs, perhaps, in Rogier van der Weyden's "Medici Madonna" of about 1450 in Frankfurt (Fig. 19).[51] In this painting, angels pull aside the curtains of a tent to reveal a standing Virgin nursing the Christ Child. It can hardly be coincidental that this tent echoes the appearance of cloth coverings of the Host in hanging tabernacles.[52] The word *tabernaculum*, in fact, originally signified the "veil or small tent of cloth" that covered Host containers suspended over the altar.[53]

In the Gothic period, Host receptacles became more and more elaborate. By the fifteenth century, the favorite shape in the north was the monumental sacrament house in the shape of a tower, such as the example of c. 1450 in Louvain (Fig. 20).[54] Since towers are naturally inaccessible, this form developed logically from the need to display the reserved Host in a locked and unreachable place.[55]

The tower is, however, also one of Mary's many epithets.[56] Early Netherlandish pictures of the Madonna often portray her in confined interior spaces that may parallel the inner enclosure of a sacrament house. Philip has suggested, for instance, that the *Annunciation* of the Ghent Altarpiece (Fig. 89) occurs in the high, inaccessible rooms of a tower.[57] Similarly, the remote, confined room of Jan's Lucca *Madonna* (Fig. 6) may deliberately evoke an association with the enclosed space that houses the Host in a tower-tabernacle.

Elsewhere, as in Memling's *Madonna and Child with Angels* in Washington (Fig. 21),[58] towers in the landscape behind the Virgin may intentionally recall this association. Memling's regal figure occupies a space that may also be a tower room, since it is elevated above the background landscape. With her erect posture and shelf-like lap, furthermore, this Madonna may also be intended to recall the Eyckian analogy between the Virgin and the altar.

Rogier's Thyssen *Madonna and Child* (Fig. 16) portrays neither a tower nor a cloth covering of the Host. The architectural decoration of its niche, however, bears an astonishing resemblance to a third type of tabernacle. Recesses in church walls, known as aumbries, are documented throughout the Middle Ages. They were often used to display locked receptacles that contained the consecrated Host,[59] and were common in Flanders from the fourteenth century on.[60]

Two preserved Flemish aumbries of the fifteenth century are particularly close to Rogier's niche: the examples in the church at Wenduyne and in the chapel of Sainte-Vérone in the vicinity of Leefdael (Figs. 22 and 23).[61] The floral motifs, finials, and blind arcades in Rogier's panel closely

22. Aumbry, height 80¼″ (204 cm).
Wenduyne.

23. Aumbry, height c. 51¼″ (c. 130 cm).
Leefdael, Sainte Vérone.

24. Jan Provost. Altarpiece of the Virgin Enthroned, center panel, 60⅞ x 56⅛″ (154.5 x 142.5 cm). Lisbon, Museu Nacional de Arte Antiga.

resemble their counterparts in both tabernacles. In place of the locked doors, however, Rogier has depicted the nursing Virgin. The niche in Rogier's painting echoes the appearance of the aumbries that displayed the container of the Host, because it frames the woman who was the sacred vessel of Christ's body.

Later Netherlandish portrayals of the Virgin and Child sometimes express Mary's association with both the altar and the tabernacle even more explicitly. In the center panel of an altarpiece by Jan Provost in Lisbon (Fig. 24),[62] for instance, the Virgin's throne rests on an actual altar. Devotional figures crowd around Mary, the "living altar," who holds the Infant on a white cloth above the corporal that covers the altar below her. Behind the Virgin, angels part the curtains of a veiled tent that recalls the tabernacle in Rogier's "Medici Madonna" (Fig. 19).

Although it may lack the subtlety of the other paintings we have studied in this chapter, Provost's panel combines their various meanings in a single image. It portrays Mary as the living counterpart of the altar-table, on which the "bread of life" rests during Mass. It explains that the mother who housed Christ's body in her womb parallels the tabernacle that contains the Eucharistic wafers. By means of these analogies, it simultaneously extolls the Virgin and dramatizes her relationship to the only two objects in the church that support and contain the consecrated Host.

NOTES TO CHAPTER I

1. The standard study of the history of the altar is still Braun. For additional bibliography on the subject, see "Altar" in *Oxford Dictionary*, 41.

2. For these tabernacles, see below, Ch. I, nn. 52–55 and the accompanying text.

3. For an introduction to the vast subject of Marian symbolism in medieval and Renaissance art, see W. Braunfels, "Maria, Marienbild: IV, Das Marienbild in der Kunst des Westens bis zum Konzil von Trient," in *Lexikon*, III, 182ff. In addition to the bibliography cited there on 198, see the valuable summaries of the subject in Hirn, 435ff. and Purtle, Ch. 1, 3ff. Also useful, in spite of its feminist bias, is the recent study by Warner.

4. Städelsches Kunstinstitut; Friedländer, I, pl. 52. See Snyder, "Chronology," 297, for a convenient summary of opinions on the dates of all of the Eyckian paintings cited here. The panel derives its title from the fact that it was once in the collection of the Duke of Lucca. Panofsky, n. 184³, has suggested that it may have been commissioned by "... a member of the Lucchese colony at Bruges of which Giovanni Arnolfini, the faithful client of Jan van Eyck, was the most prominent member."

5. E.g., Panofsky, 144. See Purtle, 113f., for further implications of this theme.

6. Ch. IX, lines 53–4 (Lutz and Perdrizet, 21): "Thronus veri Salomonis est Beatissima Virgo Maria,/ In quo residebat Jesus Christus, vera Sophia." This passage is cited in Forsyth, *Throne*, 27. For the problematic authorship and date of the *Speculum Humanae Salvationis*, see Lutz and Perdrizet, 247ff., where it is attributed to Ludolphus of Saxony about 1324.

7. For the sources of the Throne of Solomon, see especially Forsyth, *Throne*, 24ff. In addition to the references that she lists in nn. 61–64 on 25f., see Bourassé, 213ff., and H. Laag, "Thron," in *Lexikon*, IV, 304f.

8. For this panel, in the Staatliche Museen, see Stange, II, 128f., fig. 163; F. Piper, "Maria als Thron Salomos und ihre Tugenden bei der Verkündigung," *Jahrbücher für Kunstwissenschaft*, V, 1873, 97ff.; and Berlin, Staatliche Museen, *Beschreibendes Verzeichnis der Gemälde*, 523f. Other schematic versions include the miniature on fol. 2 of Paris, Bibliothèque Nationale, ms. fr. 9220, second half of the thirteenth century (F. Wormald, "The Throne of Solomon and St. Edward's Chair," in *De Artibus Opuscula*

XL. Essays in Honor of Erwin Panofsky, ed. M. Meiss, New York, 1961, 532ff., pl. 175, fig. 1, and the full-page frontispiece of Gautier de Coincy's *Miracles de Nostre Dame* of c. 1325–50 (Paris, Bibliothèque Nationale, ms. fr. 24541, fol. Av.; *ibid.*, 536ff., pl. 176, fig. 4).

9. Church of St. Jean. For a recent discussion of the relationship of the Rolin *Madonna* (Fig. 11 here) to Mosan statues of this type, see Van Buren, 622f., figs. 4–5, with the example in Liège reproduced as fig. 6. For the Liège Madonna, see also R. Didier, "La Sculpture mosane du XIᵉ au milieu du XIIIᵉ siècle," in Cologne, Schnütgen Museum, *Rhein und Maas. Kunst und Kultur 800–1400*, 1973, II, 414 and figs. 14–17. Other major Belgian examples are illustrated in Borchgrave d'Altena, 65ff., figs. 49–101. For the French versions of these statues, see especially Forsyth, *Throne*, with a catalogue beginning on 156.

10. L. B. Philip has frequently proposed this analogy in her graduate courses on Van Eyck. Cf. Purtle, 103, where Mary's lap in this painting is compared to a "block of stone." For the parallel of the Infant Christ on a white cloth to the Eucharist on the corporal, see also Philip, "Kölnische Kreuzigung," 223, n. 2.

11. See Panofsky, 143f., and Purtle, 114ff. for various interpretations of the meanings of these objects.

12. For additional levels of meaning of the basin, see Panofsky, 143, and Purtle, 115ff.

13. *Oxford Dictionary*, 1093.

14. For liturgical niches and the meaning of the washing of the priest's hands, see below, Ch. II, nn. 9–11 and the accompanying text. Cf. the basin in the niche of the *Annunciation* of the Ghent Altarpiece, Fig. 89 here.

15. This analogy has long been recognized by L. B. Philip in her courses on Van Eyck. Cf. Baldass, 52; Blum, 12; Blum, "Symbolic Invention," 104; and Purtle, 140. For this painting, in the Staatliche Kunstsammlungen in Dresden, see also Friedländer, I, pl. 54–55.

16. Cf. Blum, 12, and Purtle, 90f. For this painting, in the Groeninge Museum, see also Friedländer, I, pl. 23.

17. For this manuscript (Bibliothèque Nationale, ms. lat. 18014), see Meiss, 334ff., with this miniature (fol. 139) reproduced as

fig. 128. For other examples of the Duke of Berry praying at an altar in the *Petites Heures,* see *ibid.,* 88ff., with numerous illustrations. Cf. the discussion of this miniature and its relationship to the Rolin *Madonna* in Purtle, 64f.

18. Musée du Louvre; Friedländer, I, pl. 51. For attempts to identify the palatial setting in this painting, see, e.g., Panofsky, 139; Snyder, "Jan van Eyck and the Madonna of Chancellor Nicolas Rolin," 165f.; and Philip, 198. Most recently, Van Buren, 619f., has interpreted the setting as a watchtower, in connection with the twelfth-century writings of Honorius of Autun.

19. *Ibid.,* 631f. Cf. the discussion in Purtle, 60ff.

20. E.g., Philip, 94, and Purtle, 14.

21. See especially Guarducci, 280ff., where the origins of the legend are traced to Johannes Malalas, *Chronographia,* Book X (Migne, *P.G.,* XCVII, 357). Cf. the unsigned article, "Augustus," in *Lexikon,* I, 225f.

22. Voragine, 49 (chapter on the Nativity), and Lutz and Perdrizet, 19 (Ch. VIII, lines 85–94). The *Golden Legend* probably dates between 1255 and 1266; see *Oxford Dictionary,* 579. For the date and authorship of the *Speculum,* see above, Ch. I, n. 6.

23. Staatliche Museen; Friedländer, II, #38. For earlier depictions of the legend, with the Virgin and Child in half length, see Meiss, 233ff., figs. 815–20, and Meiss, *Limbourgs,* 140, figs. 395–97.

24. E.g., Pseudo-Methodius of Olympus, *Sermo de Simeone et Anna XIV* (Migne, *P.G.,* XVIII, 382B): "animatum panis illius vitae altare." According to Guarducci, 284, this sermon was published under the name of Methodius no later than the eighth century. For other Byzantine sources for this idea, see especially *ibid.,* 284, and Bourassé, 250, where precise citations are lacking. Cf. Hirn, 473, who has mentioned this analogy with no sources at all: ". . . the table which bears the holy bread is also a symbol of that woman who bore the Divine Child . . ." See also Hagar, 29, who has discussed this tradition in relation to a fresco of about 1280–1300, in Subiaco (his fig. 23), in which the altar below a half-length Virgin actually replaces her lap. I am grateful to Lotte Brand Philip for bringing this example to my attention.

25. See Guarducci, 283, and Bourassé, 249ff.

26. E.g., Pseudo-Bernard (thirteenth century), *In Antiphonam Salve Regina Sermo III* (Migne, *P.L.,* CLXXXIV, 1069C): "[Ipsa] mensa est."

27. Ch. V, lines 5–32 (Lutz and Perdrizet, 12). See *ibid.,* 188, where this passage is described as a deformation of a legend in Plutarch that was known in the Middle Ages through Valerius Maximus. Valerius' version is printed on 188 of *ibid.,* along with a discussion of the problematic origin of the analogy between the golden altar and the Virgin.

28. For this famous treatise, see especially Bodenstedt.

29. Ch. V, lines 27–32 (Lutz and Perdrizet, 12):

Pulchre Maria est per mensam solis
    praefigurata,
Quia per eam coelestis esca nobis
    est collata;
Nam ipsa filiam Dei Jesum Christum
    nobis generavit,
Qui nos suo corpore et sanguine
    refocillavit.
Benedicta sit ista beatissima mensa,
Per quam collata est nobis esca tam
    salubris et tam immensa!

30. *Vita Christi,* Part I, Ch. II, *De Salute Generis Humani et Nativitate Mariae* (Ludolphus, I, 22); "Et pulchre per mensam Maria est figurata, quia per eam coelestis esca nobis est collata, nam ipsa Filium Dei Jesum Christum nobis generavit, qui nos suo corpore et sanguine refocillavit."

31. For the influence of these books, see especially Lutz and Perdrizet, 287ff., and Bodenstedt, 53ff.

32. Friedländer, I, pl. 78. For a proposed reconstruction of the triptych to which this signed and dated panel originally belonged, see Lane, "Petrus Christus," and C. Eisler, *Paintings from the Samuel H. Kress Collection: European Schools Excluding Italian,* Oxford, 1977, 52, text fig. 17.

33. See Lane, "Petrus Christus," 392f., for the possible Italian origin of Christus' inclusion of standing saints on either side of the enthroned Virgin.

34. For altar curtains, see Hirn, 114, and below, Ch. II, nn. 44–46 and the accompanying text.

35. Hirn, 473.

36. Forsyth, *Throne,* 49ff. For the texts of this play, see Young, II, 29ff. See also below, Ch. II, nn. 66–67 and the accompanying text.

37. E.g., in a fourteenth-century text from Rouen (Young, II, 43, with similar fifteenth-century texts cited on 437). Cf. Forsyth, *Throne,* 57 and 57, n. 86.

38. *Ibid.,* 57; this section of Forsyth's book is based on her earlier "Magi," 215ff.

39. Forsyth, *Throne,* fig. 43, and P. Lasko, *Ars Sacra, 800–1200,* Harmondsworth, 1972, fig. 121. A similar example occurs on the twelfth-century tympanum of the right portal on the northern facade of Reims Cathedral (E. Moreau-Nélaton, *La Cathédral de Reims,* Paris, 1915, pl. 109–10).

40. See, e.g., the versions by Memling in which worshipers kneel beside Mary's throne as Canon van der Paele kneels in Jan's panel (fig. 10 here): Friedländer, VIa, #9, 10, 63, and 66.

41. E.g., K. M. Birkmeyer, "Notes on the Two Earliest Paintings by Rogier van der Weyden," *Art Bulletin,* XLIV, 1962, 330. The panel is usually dated early, c. 1430–32; see *ibid.,* 329, and Panofsky, 251. An early date is also presumed by J. L. Ward, who believes the panel to be by Campin, in "A New Attribution for the 'Madonna Enthroned' in the Thyssen Bornemisza Collection," *Art Bulletin,* L, 1968, 354ff. For this panel, see also Friedländer, II, #8, and Davies, 222f.

42. Panofsky, 146. For Mary's role as the Church in paintings of this period, see also below, Ch. 3.

43. For the Virgin as tabernacle, see especially Hirn, 454 and 550, n. 53; Bourassé, 156ff.; Philip, 93; and Purtle, 6.

44. Amadeus of Lausanne, 64f. (Homily I, lines 183–87): "Urna aurea beata est Maria. . . . Haec urna manna reconditum habuit quae panem angelorum, qui de caelo descendit et dat vitam mundo, sacrosancto gessit in utero." Cf. the English translation of this homily in Bernard of Clairvaux and Amadeus of Lausanne, *Magnificat,* 61ff.

45. Mone, 309, #524, lines 1–6:

Salve mater salvatoris,
vas electum, vas honoris,
vas coelestis gratiae;
Ab aeterno vas provisum,
vas insigne, vas excisum
manu sapientiae.

Cf. the rhymed translation in D. S. Wrangham, *The Liturgical Poetry of Adam of St. Victor,* II, London, 1881, 219, #LXXIII.

46. Book I, ch. iii, 25 (Barthélemy, I, 53). This passage is quoted in Hirn, 163, and Philip, 96, n. 195. Cf. the translation in Neale and Webb, 56. For the popularity of Durandus' treatise in the fifteenth century, see especially Ringbom, 40.

47. Ch. X, lines 45–46 (Lutz and Perdrizet, 22): "Arca et urnam auream cum manna

continebat,/ Et Maria verum manna coeli nobis offerebat." Cf. the similar idea in Ch. XLV, lines 39–40 (*ibid.,* 96).

48. See, e.g., Mone, II, 270, #507, lines 161–62 and 430, #610, lines 64–70 (both of the fourteenth to fifteenth centuries), and 434, #612, line 13 (fifteenth century). Cf. Hirn, 321 and 550, n. 53.

49. For this type of shrine, see Hirn, 321f.; Fries, 5ff.; Philip, 93; W. Braunfels, "Maria, Marienbild," in *Lexikon,* III, 193f.; and, most recently, Baumer, 239ff.

50. *Ibid.,* fig. 14. Holes in the body of the Lord and in the cross indicate where the dove of the Holy Spirit and the body of Christ must once have been attached. See Hirn, 321, and Fries, 51, for the sources of Mary as the container of the Trinity.

51. For this panel, preserved in the Städelsches Kunstinstitut and usually dated about 1450, see Friedländer, II, #21; Panofsky, 274f.; M. G. Lanckorońska, "Die Medici-Madonna des Rogier van der Weyden," *Wallraf-Richartz-Jahrbuch,* XXXI, 1969, 25ff.; and Davies, 212f., who has included a convenient summary of the arguments regarding its alleged association with the Medici family.

52. See the reproductions of such tents in Raible, figs. 34–36, and Maffei, fig. 10. This symbolism in Rogier's painting was recognized in an unpublished M.A. thesis by S. L. Zilber, "The Tent: an Iconographic Image in Northern European Art of the late Middle Ages and Early Renaissance," Yale University, 1978, 17. Similar tents occur in two works attributed to Campin: the *Enthroned Madonna with Saints and Donors* drawing at the Louvre in Paris and the *Holy Trinity* panel at the Hermitage in Leningrad (Friedländer, II, #72a and 65).

53. Van Dijk and Walker, 35. For these hanging tabernacles, see also Raible, 162ff.; Maffei, 50ff.; and King, 121ff. and 132.

54. Collegiate Church of St. Peter. For this example, which is the earliest preserved sacrament house in Belgium, see Maffei, 101, fig. 25; King, 108; and Philip, fig. 22. For Host reservation in the Netherlands, see especially Maffei.

55. For the tower-tabernacle, see especially Hirn, 159ff.; Reusens, II, 273ff.; Raible, 152ff. and 193ff.; Maffei, 91ff.; Van Dijk and Walker, 27ff.; and King, 104ff.

56. For the analogy between the tower and Mary, see, e.g., Hirn, 444ff. The *Speculum Humanae Salvationis,* for instance, compares her to the tower of David (Ch. VI, lines 83ff.; Lutz and Perdrizet, 15).

57. Philip, 83f.

58. National Gallery of Art; Friedländer, VIa, #60.

59. For the prevalence of aumbries throughout Europe in the Middle Ages, see especially Van Dijk and Walker, 40ff. According to these authors, aumbries were common even before the 1215 Lateran decree that the consecrated Host must be preserved in a locked place; their book is, in fact, a denial of Dix's claim that aumbries resulted directly from this decree (G. Dix, *A Detection of Aumbries,* London, 1942.) Cf. also the discussions of the problem by Raible, 172ff., on which Dix's book is based; Maffei, 75ff.; and King, 95ff.

60. Reusens, II, 272f.; Maffei, 75ff.; and King, 101.

61. The aumbry at Wenduyne is reproduced in Maffei, fig. 12, and the one in Sainte-Vérone appears in Reusens, II, 273, fig. 1. For additional examples of Flemish aumbries of this period, see especially Maffei, 77ff. Although their architectural decoration is simpler, Rogier's other Madonnas in niches may also convey this symbolism: the *Madonna in Red* at the Prado (Friedländer, II, Supp. 132) and the *Standing Madonna* in the Kunsthistorisches Museum in Vienna (*ibid., #7*).

62. Museu Nacional de Arte Antiga, early sixteenth century; Friedländer, IX, part 2, #123. I am grateful to Lotte Brand Philip for bringing this example to my attention.

25. Robert Campin, Mérode Altarpiece, center panel: *Annunciation,* 25¼ x 24¾″ (64 x 63 cm). New York, Metropolitan Museum of Art, The Cloisters Collection, Purchase.

II
Incarnation, Transubstantiation, and the Rituals of Christmas

The Transubstantiation is one of the central mysteries of Catholic dogma. It occurs at the dramatic climax of the Mass. According to Catholic thought, this is the moment when the Holy Spirit descends over the altar and changes the wafer and the wine of the Eucharist into the body and blood of Christ.

In Catholic art and literature, this mystical transformation was frequently compared with the moment in which the word of God became flesh in the womb of the Virgin. Since the Holy Spirit causes the conception of the "living bread," Christ, at the Incarnation, this event parallels the daily miracle that occurs during the Eucharistic rite performed at the altar. As Hirn has written, "When the young woman became a mother without losing her virginity, this was due to the fact that the Holy Ghost had 'overshadowed' her; and when the bread is transformed into a God without changing its shape, the Holy Ghost has descended over the Mass-table."[1]

The association of Christ's Incarnation with the ceremony of Transubstantiation has a long and complex history. Katzenellenbogen has traced the source of the relationship between these two miracles to Christ's words in John 6:51: "I am the living bread which came down from heaven: if any man eat of this bread, he shall live forever: and the bread that I will give is my flesh, which I will give for the life of the world."[2] In a comprehensive discussion of the continual references to this analogy throughout the Middle Ages, Nilgen has recognized that any scene of Christ's Infancy can be used to convey the mystery of his Incarnation.[3] Some subjects, however, lend themselves more easily than others to Eucharistic interpretations.

In early Netherlandish painting, more Annunciations occur than any other subject from Christ's Infancy, although there are also many panels of

41

the Nativity and the Adoration of the Magi. The Flight into Egypt, on the other hand, appears in only one of the preserved series of Infancy scenes,[4] and no major single panel of it remains. Although it is possible that additional subjects of this cycle no longer survive, it can be no coincidence that the most common preserved Infancy themes are precisely the ones that are related most closely to the daily Mass and to liturgical ceremonies of the Christmas season. This chapter will consider how some of the major early Netherlandish Incarnation scenes dramatize this relationship.

Robert Campin's Mérode Annunciation

In most early Netherlandish Annunciations, Gabriel appears to the Virgin in a small room of a simple Flemish house. These rooms and the specific objects in them have been the object of much scholarly debate, especially in the case of the central panel of Robert Campin's Mérode Altarpiece in New York (Fig. 25).[5] Scholars have often described the realistic setting of this Annunciation as a "domestic interior." It is, however, no less sacramental than the room in Campin's *Madonna and Child Before a Fire Screen* (Fig. 1).

The story of the Annunciation is told in the Gospel of Saint Luke (Luke 1:26–38). In this account, there is no description of its location, although one statement suggests an interior setting: ". . . the angel came in unto her. . . ." (Luke 1:28). Nothing in Luke's passage, however, can have inspired the meticulously detailed rooms that appear in the Mérode *Annunciation* and in most other early Netherlandish interpretations of the event. Even the most descriptive late medieval treatises on Christ's life offer no explanation for these intimate settings. In the popular *Meditations on the Life of Christ* of the thirteenth century, for instance, the author wrote only that the angel appeared to Mary ". . . in a room of her little house."[6] Here, again, there is no description of the room or any objects in it.

Scholars have recognized that the symbolic details of the Mérode *Annunciation* identify it as a sanctuary.[7] The niche behind the angel, for instance, with its laver and hanging towel, does not belong in a domestic interior. Gottlieb has identified it as a liturgical niche, or *piscina,* an object mentioned above in connection with Jan's Lucca *Madonna* (Fig. 6).[8] The function of the *piscina* is illustrated in a miniature of 1455 in Utrecht (Fig. 26),[9] where it appears in its traditional place at the right of the altar. Durandus clarified the symbolic purification of the ceremony enacted at the *piscina* when he wrote, "Near to the Altar, which signifieth Christ, is the Piscina, or Lavacrum, that is, the Pity of Christ, in which the

26. *Priest Washing His Hands,* Pontifical. Utrecht, University Library.

priest washeth his hands, thereby denoting, that by Baptism and Penance we are purged from the filth of sin."[10]

In Campin's painting, the niche contains a laver like the one in the miniature rather than the basin that appears in the Lucca *Madonna.* A basin and a laver occur together, however, in the niche of the *Annunciation* of the Ghent Altarpiece (Fig. 89).[11] All three niches must share the same implications.

Scholars have identified the table of the Mérode *Annunciation* as an altar, in a logical application of the table-altar analogy that Nilgen has recognized in Epiphany scenes.[12] Gottlieb has proposed, moreover, that the presence of the tiny Christ Child, who enters the room on the rays of the Holy Spirit, characterizes the space as a tabernacle containing the body of Christ.[13] The angel's flowing white alb and the amice around his neck are liturgical garments that also contribute to the sanctity of the setting. His stole, moreover, draped over his left shoulder and tied under his right arm, identifies him as a deacon at Mass.[14] In Campin's painting, therefore, the room is both a sanctuary that contains the altar and a tabernacle that encloses the Eucharist. Its space is just as sacramental as that of the pictures of the enthroned Madonna considered in the previous chapter.

27. Master of Catherine of Cleves, *Annunciation, Hours of Katharina van Lochorst,* 7½ x 5″ (19 x 12.9 cm). Münster, Westfälisches Landesmuseum für Kunst and Kulturgeschichte.

A rarely published miniature of about 1450, in the *Hours of Katharina van Lochorst* in Münster (Fig. 27), substantiates the above interpretation.[15] The painter of this scene was the innovative Master of Catherine of Cleves, who occasionally adapted compositions by Campin.[16] Although Pieper has discussed the artist's dependence on the Mérode *Annunciation* for the figure of Mary in the miniature,[17] he has not explained the implications of the major alterations of the setting. The differences between the two scenes, however, illustrate the Cleves Master's desire to express the sacramental meaning of Campin's space in a more literal way.

No liturgical niche is necessary in the miniature, since its interior is clearly a sanctuary. An actual altar in the apse behind the figures replaces the table-altar between Mary and the angel in Campin's painting. Significantly, the two figures again appear on either side of it. As in the Mérode *Annunciation,* this space is also a tabernacle, in which a tiny figure of the Infant Christ descends on the rays of the Holy Spirit. A tent above Mary's throne enhances the association with a tabernacle; as in Rogier's "Medici Madonna" (Fig. 19), it refers to her as the living receptacle of Christ. Finally, the angel wears a jeweled cope over his alb, as do the subministers at Mass.[18] By means of these changes, the Cleves Master created a literal reinterpretation of the implications of Campin's painting.

The ecclesiastical setting of the Cleves miniature continues a long tradition in manuscript illumination of placing the Annunciation in a church interior.[19] This tradition recurs only rarely in early Netherlandish painting, as in Jan's *Annunciation* in Washington (Fig. 28).[20] Here, in a setting far more unified and realistic than in the Cleves miniature, the interior is immediately recognizable as a church, even though its combination of Romanesque and Gothic architectural motifs may be less logical than symbolic.[21] In this remarkably detailed panel, Gabriel's elaborate liturgical vestments again characterize him as a participant in the sacred ritual of Mass.

Similarly garbed angels appear, however, in all of the Annunciations of the period, even though the settings in these panels look more like bedrooms than sanctuaries. The standard formula for the representation of the theme in the later part of the fifteenth century developed from panels such as Rogier's Louvre *Annunciation* and the left wing of his Columba Altarpiece in Munich (Figs. 29 and 30).[22] In both of these rhythmic compositions, Mary kneels at a prie-dieu in front of a bed and pauses in her reading to listen to Gabriel's message. The angel in each painting wears

28. Jan van Eyck, *Annunciation,* 36⅝ x 14⅝″ (93 x 37 cm). Washington, D.C., National Gallery of Art, Andrew Mellon Collection.

carefully portrayed church vestments, which are most elaborate in the version at the Louvre.

Various details in each of these interiors make it clear that they are just as sacred as the rooms of Campin's Mérode *Annunciation* and Jan's panel in Washington. In the panel at the Louvre, for instance, a bronze laver rests in a basin on top of a cabinet behind the angel. Although these instruments of washing look less out of place here than does the *piscina* in the Mérode *Annunciation*, they may also have a liturgical function. Similar objects rest above a drain on the right side of the altar in the *Mass of Saint Gregory* in Brussels (Fig. 87).[23] Although no niche appears in this scene, the laver and basin would certainly have been used for the washing of the priest's hands, as in the miniature in Utrecht (Fig. 26). In Rogier's Louvre *Annunciation*, these objects are perfectly logical as daily washing utensils, but they also contribute to the identification of the space as a sanctuary.

The simpler interior of Rogier's Columba *Annunciation* contains no laver or basin. In this case, it is the architecture that seems strange for a domestic setting. What bedroom of the period would have had a barrel-vaulted ceiling or a rose window above the bed? Both features, however, would have been perfectly suitable in a church.[24] Here, then, as in the Mérode *Annunciation* and the other early Netherlandish Annunciations in interiors, the symbolic details identify the sanctity of the space.

One additional connection between the Annunciation and church rituals remains to be considered: a liturgical drama that was popular in Belgium and Holland throughout the fifteenth century.[25] The *Missa Aurea*, or Golden Mass, was performed at Tournai as early as 1231,[26] and various texts of it remain from the late Gothic period. A sixteenth-century version from Tournai, for instance, includes a description of its staging. Two curtained platforms supported boys who were dressed as Mary and Gabriel. At the beginning of the Mass, Mary's curtain was opened, and Gabriel was revealed during the singing of *Gloria in Excelsis*. Later in the ceremony, an image of a dove was lowered over the platform of the kneeling Virgin.[27]

McNamee has proposed that this drama influenced some of the details in a French painting of about 1450, the *Annunciation* in Aix-en-Provence,[28] and Purtle has argued that the positions and gestures of the figures in Jan's Washington *Annunciation* (Fig. 28) echo the actions of the performers in it.[29] Since texts of this play from Belgium attest to its continual performance there, the Flemish painters were certainly familiar with it. The doves that hover so concretely over Mary's head and literally "overshadow" her in many Annunciations of the period, as, for instance, in

29. Rogier van der Weyden, *Annunciation,* 33⅞ x 36¼″ (86 x 92 cm). Paris, Musée du Louvre.

30. Rogier van der Weyden, Columba Altarpiece, left wing: *Annunciation,* 54⅜ x 27½″ (138 x 70 cm). Munich, Alte Pinakothek.

Jan's version in the Ghent Altarpiece (Fig. 89), may even recall the doves that were lowered over her platform during the ceremony.[30]

It is also possible that these sculptural doves echo the Host receptacles shaped like doves that descended over the altar-table at the moment of Transubstantiation.[31] The fundamental association of the Annunciation with this central mystery of Mass, in fact, is strong enough to explain its popularity as a subject in altarpieces of the period. It is worth noting, however, that the Golden Mass was performed not on the Feast of the Annunciation on March 25, but on Ember Wednesday of Advent, immediately preceding the Christmas season.[32] The frequency of the Annunciation in early Netherlandish painting may also be a result of the need to illustrate this prelude to the celebration of the birth of Christ.

In addition to the Annunciation, only three subjects of Christ's Infancy appear with any frequency in early Netherlandish painting: the Nativity, the Adoration of the Magi, and the Presentation in the Temple. All three events were commemorated by major feasts that closely follow each other in the church year: Christmas (December 25), Epiphany (January 6), and Candlemas (February 2). Their popularity in the altarpieces of the period may derive from the desire for pictorial parallels of these ceremonies. It is necessary, therefore, to explain how they were dramatized in some of the major surviving early Netherlandish examples.

Hugo van der Goes's Berlin Nativity

The numerous Nativities of the period portray silent vigils in which kneeling figures adore the newborn Infant. Christ, who lies either on the ground or in a rectangular manger, is usually the main focus of the composition. In the version by Hugo van der Goes in Berlin (Fig. 31),[33] for instance, Mary, Joseph, and adoring angels crowd around the central manger, while awestruck shepherds rush in at the left. Two enigmatic half-length male figures in the foreground pull curtains aside to reveal the scene behind them. The complex meaning of this mystical image cannot be understood through reference to the Biblical account alone.

The story of the Nativity and Adoration of the Shepherds occurs in the Gospels only in Luke 2:1–16. In verse 6 of this passage, Luke describes the shepherds' arrival at the scene of Christ's birth: "And they came with haste, and found Mary, and Joseph, and the babe lying in a manger." Whereas this statement may explain the forward movement of the two shepherds at the left of Hugo's painting, nothing in Luke's description

31. Hugo van der Goes, *Nativity*, 38¼ x 96½" (97 x 245 cm). Berlin, Staatliche Museen Preussischer Kulturbesitz, Gemäldegalerie.

32. *Nativity,* c. 7½ x 9⅜" (c. 19 x 23.7 cm). Munich, Bayerisches Nationalmuseum.

accounts for the angels beside the manger. The author of the *Meditations of the Life of Christ,* however, described how all of the angels flew to earth to adore the Child when they heard of his birth.[34] Yet this source contains no explanation for the half-length figures in the foreground.

Scholars have frequently explained the kneeling position of the Virgin in Nativities of this period as a result of Saint Brigitta's vision of the miracle, for earlier northern versions of the theme had portrayed Mary on a mattress in the Byzantine manner.[35] Whereas Brigitta's description may be the source for Hugo's kneeling Madonna, it includes no clues to the other details of Hugo's picture.

As I have demonstrated elsewhere, Hugo's Berlin *Nativity* evokes the parallel between the Incarnation and the Transubstantiation by dramatizing the traditional relationship between the manger and the altar.[36] The sheaf of grain just below the manger in this painting refers to Christ as "the living bread which came down from heaven" (John 6:51). It visually underscores the prominently placed rectangular manger, where the Infant Christ on a white cloth parallels the wafer of the Host on the corporal on the altar. Mary and Joseph kneel on either side of the manger here, in the same way that they often flank a high altar-table in earlier versions of the theme: for example, a fourteenth-century German panel in Munich (Fig. 32).[37] Since altars like this have no place in realistic interpretations of the setting of Christ's birth, however, Hugo and the other painters of the period had to find alternative ways to express the sanctity of the space.

Throughout the Middle Ages, writers equated the Christ Child with the Host and the manger with the altar. Walafrid Strabo (d. 849), for example, declared, ". . . placed in the manger, that is the body of Christ on the altar. . . ."[38] This analogy appears in the Christmas liturgy, in passages such as the Benediction formula of Christmas Mass in the Gregorian Sacramentary: "And He [God the Father] made Him, who is the bread of the angels in the manger of the church, be food for the faithful creatures. . . ."[39]

The manger-altar analogy led to numerous miracles in which the Host was transformed into an image of the Infant Christ at the moment of elevation. Literal depictions of these miracles occur frequently in Gothic art.[40] The symbolic Transubstantiation portrayed in such miracles also occurs in the Berlin *Nativity,* where the Christ Child lying on the manger explains the meaning of the consecrated Host to the worshiper.

The sheaf of wheat in Hugo's picture identifies the space as a sanctuary, or the *domus panis,* which Gregory described in his discussion of the meaning of the word "Bethlehem": "He is also for good reasons born in Bethlehem, for Bethlehem means house of bread. . . ."[41] Hugo used grain in the same way to identify the space in the center panel of his Portinari Altarpiece (Fig. 33),[42] where it parallels the outstretched body of the Infant Christ. This motif reappears in later panels executed under Hugo's influence, such as Gerard David's *Nativity* in New York (Fig. 34).[43] Here, Joseph has laid his cane on it in the lower right corner. He joins Mary in a ritualistic adoration of the Infant, who lies between them on a horizontally placed manger that recalls the altars in scenes such as the one in the Munich panel (Fig. 32).

In the Berlin *Nativity,* Hugo reinforced the manger-altar analogy with the inclusion of curtains that part to reveal the scene. As mentioned above, curtains hanging from rods on either side of the altar were used to conceal the mystery of the Transubstantiation.[44] These curtains were opened at the moment of elevation to reveal the transformed Host.[45] This

33. Hugo van der Goes, Portinari Altarpiece, 98 x 226″ (249 x 574 cm). Florence, Uffizi.

34. Gerard David, *Nativity with Donors and Patron Saints,* center panel: *Nativity,* 35¼ x 28″ (89.6 x 71.1 cm). New York, Metropolitan Museum of Art, Jules S. Bache Collection, 1949.

is illustrated in the Netherlandish *Mass of Saint Giles* of about 1500 in London (Fig. 35).[46] Altar curtains often appear in Gothic Nativities that depict the manger as an actual altar, as in the *Incarnation* Window at Chartres Cathedral of about 1150 (Fig. 36).[47] In these scenes, as in Hugo's painting, they reveal the Child just as altar curtains disclosed the transformed Host to the congregation.

Hugo's curtains, however, may also refer to a liturgical drama performed on Christmas Day: the *Officium Pastorum,* or Shepherds' Play. In this drama, clergymen impersonating shepherds approached the altar, where a *praesepe* with an image of the Virgin and Child was hidden be-

35. Master of Saint Giles,
Mass of Saint Giles, 24¼ x
18″ (61.5 x 45.5 cm).
London, The National
Gallery.

36. *Incarnation* Window, detail:
Nativity. Chartres Cathedral.

hind curtains. At the proper dramatic moment, two priests representing midwives opened the curtains to reveal the figures behind them.[48] The parted curtains in Hugo's painting may correspond to the ones in this play. The shepherds who rush in from the left toward the manger-altar, moreover, may echo the movement of the shepherds who approached the altar in the *Officium Pastorum.*

Hugo's two foreground figures certainly cannot be identified with the priests who separated the curtains in the Shepherds' Play. Scholars usually interpret them as prophets unveiling the New Testament scene.[49] There is, however, another Christmas ceremony that may provide a clue to their identities.

The *Ordo Prophetarum* often immediately preceded the Shepherds' Play and sometimes served as a prologue to more complex Nativity dramas.[50] In this introductory ceremony, a procession of prophets quoted their own writings as announcements of the coming of Christ. The first two prophets of the *Ordo Prophetarum,* and often the only two in the shortest versions of it, were Isaiah and Jeremiah.[51] In Hugo's painting, the figure on the left is probably Isaiah, who looks into the scene of the fulfillment of his prophecy that a Virgin would bear a son (Isaiah 7:14). The grieving, tense figure on the right may portray Jeremiah, whose tortured life was interpreted as a prefiguration of Christ's suffering.[52]

Other motifs in Hugo's picture echo this reference to Christ's death. In their unveiling of the scene, the prophets recall the visual effect of angels who reveal the effigy of the deceased with parted curtains in thirteenth- and fourteenth-century Italian tombs.[53] The shape of the manger in Hugo's painting, in fact, resembles a sarcophagus. Mangers often seem to imitate tombs in Nativities of this period (for example, in Fig. 38), since the altar symbolizes Christ's tomb as well as his manger. This combined meaning is expressed most clearly in a treatise ascribed to Germanus I, Patriarch of Constantinople (d. 733): "The altar is and is called both the manger and the sepulchre of the Lord . . ."[54] Even the previously mentioned Shepherds' Play reflects the intimate relationship between these two ideas, for its text derives from the earlier Easter plays of the Visit of the Three Maries to the Tomb, the *Visitatio Sepulchri.* Both dramas were enacted at the altar, which symbolized the manger in the Christmas plays and the tomb in the performances at Easter.[55]

Hugo's Berlin *Nativity,* therefore, portrays much more than a historical scene of Christ's birth. In this dramatic painting, the Infant Christ on the manger-altar is a visual explanation of the consecrated Host. The parted curtains reveal the Child just as altar curtains disclosed the transformed

37. Petrus Christus, *Nativity,* 50⅜ x 37¾″ (128 x 96 cm). Washington, D.C., National
Gallery of Art, Andrew Mellon Collection.

Host to the congregation. Opening these curtains, Isaiah and Jeremiah introduce the scene, as did the prophets of the liturgical plays performed at Christmas around the altar. The identities of these figures relate, respectively, to the interpretation of the altar as both manger and tomb.

Other Nativities of the period include equally strong allusions to the parallel between the Incarnation and the Transubstantiation. In Petrus Christus' earlier *Nativity* in Washington (Fig. 37), for instance, the almost concrete golden mandorla around the Christ Child imitates the paten on which the Host rests during Mass.[56] Upton has interpreted the shed in this panel as the "altar of the first Mass"; he has also noted that its two central archivolt reliefs devoted to Cain and Abel relate to the coming sacrifice of Christ, who lies directly below them.[57] Joseph's prominently placed pattens recall Moses' removal of his shoes in front of the burning bush, and thereby emphasize the sanctity of the ground in this panel.[58] The wooden roof that covers the entire foreground space, moreover, shelters the ground as a ciborium protects the altar beneath it.[59]

The most mystical portrayal of the manger-altar analogy occurs, perhaps, in Geertgen tot Sint Jans's *Nativity* in London (Fig. 38).[60] Here, the

38. Geertgen tot Sint Jans, *Nativity*, 13⅜ x 9⅞″ (34 x 25 cm). London, The National Gallery.

Christ Child lies on a manger that extends across the foreground horizontally, parallel to both the picture plane and the altar that would have been immediately below it. Even the ox and the ass in this bewitching painting are transfixed by the radiance of the glowing Infant. His placement on the sarcophagus-like manger signifies the ultimate purpose of the Nativity: the inevitable sacrifice of Christ that is repeated at every Mass. Yet Geertgen's Infant, stretched out on his manger-altar, also explains the meaning of the "living bread" of the consecrated Host. Here again, then, the painting dramatizes the meaning of the altar below it as well as the constantly celebrated miracle of Transubstantiation.

Rogier van der Weyden's Columba Altarpiece

Allusions to the connection between the Incarnation and the Transubstantiation are equally prevalent in the numerous interpretations of the Adoration of the Magi in this period. This subject occurs frequently in early Netherlandish painting as the center panel of a triptych devoted to Infancy themes, as, for instance, in Rogier's Columba Altarpiece in Munich (Fig. 39).[61] We have already considered the Eucharistic implications of the *Annunciation* on the left wing of this triptych (Fig. 30),[62] and we shall investigate the meaning of the *Presentation in the Temple* (Fig. 45) in its right wing presently. In its central *Adoration of the Magi* (Fig. 40), the Child sits on Mary's lap in front of a massive arched structure with a thatched roof. To the Virgin's right appears a small three-legged table, on which the first king has placed his gift, and an anachronistic crucifix hangs above her head on the pillar behind her.

The Adoration of the Magi is the only Infancy subject that is described by Matthew rather than Luke (Matthew 2:1–12). According to his account, a star led the three kings to the Child's birthplace, where they ". . . saw the young child with Mary his mother, and fell down and worshiped him . . ." (Matthew 2:11). The passage in the *Meditations on the Life of Christ* elaborates further: "The Magi, arriving at the holy cave, dismounted, entered, and knelt impulsively before the Boy, adoring Jesus reverently, honoring Him as King and worshipping Him as God."[63] Neither source, however, explains the specific details of Rogier's painting.

Whereas the Columba *Adoration* does portray a historical rendering of the event, it also contains numerous allusions to the traditional connection of this theme with the daily ceremony of Mass. In the early church, the faithful brought gifts of bread and wine, as well as offerings for the church, to the altar, in the ceremony before the sacrifice known as the Offertory rite.[64] Writers and artists often interpreted the Magi's presenta-

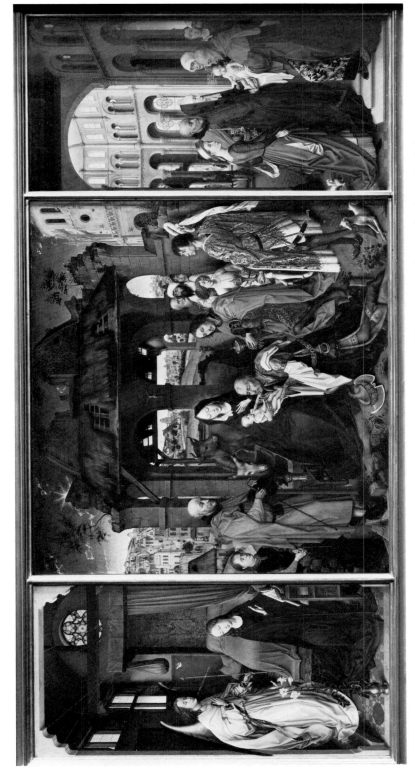

39. Rogier van der Weyden, Columba Altarpiece, 54⅜ x 115⅜" (138 x 293 cm). Munich, Alte Pinakothek.

40. Rogier van der Weyden, Columba Altarpiece, center panel: *Adoration of the Magi*, 54⅜ x 60¼" (138 x 153 cm). Munich Alte Pinakothek

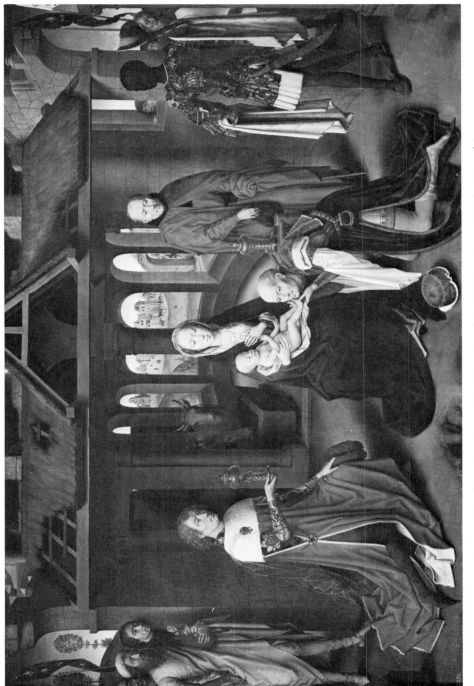

41. Hans Memling, Altarpiece of the Adoration of the Magi, center panel: *Adoration of the Magi*, 37⅜ x 57⅛" (95 x 145 cm). Madrid, Museo del Prado.

tion of gifts to the Christ Child as a parallel to this ceremony. In a sixth-century mosaic at San Vitale in Ravenna, for instance, a scene of the Magi bringing gifts appears on the hem of Theodora's robe; the empress herself carries a chalice, moreover, that suggests the wine of the Offertory. In another Ravenna mosaic of the same period at Sant' Apollinare Nuovo, similar figures echo the direction of the Offertory procession as they approach the image of the Virgin and Child to the right of the altar.[65]

By the fifteenth century, worshipers no longer participated in the Offertory rite, but they were still reminded of the Adoration of the Magi by the ceremonies performed on the Feast of the Epiphany that was celebrated on January 6. The *Officium Stellae* plays, which we considered above in relation to early Netherlandish Madonnas, were performed at Epiphany from the eleventh century into the late Middle Ages.[66] Their texts reveal the continuation of the connection between the manger and the altar. In the most elaborate versions of these plays, priests impersonating Magi assembled at the high altar and then followed a star to a second altar in the nave or transept, on which they laid their gifts. Clerics, dressed as midwives, then revealed an image of the Virgin and Child to them. The action of this play, therefore, centered on an altar that served as the manger, as it did in the *Officium Pastorum*.[67]

McNamee has suggested that the elaborate garments of the kings in Rogier's Columba *Adoration,* as well as in the other versions of the period, echo the costumes worn in the Epiphany plays.[68] He has offered this interpretation in support of Nilgen's proposal that the small table, on which the first king has placed his gift, parallels the altar on which the Offertory gifts were laid. According to Nilgen, simple tables like the one in Rogier's panel meet the realistic requirements of the scene more easily than the altar-shaped mangers that occur in earlier versions of the theme as well as in earlier Nativities (cf. Fig. 36). She has suggested, therefore, that such tables function as altars in this period.[69]

Tables like the one in the Columba *Adoration* do not, however, appear in every early Netherlandish interpretation of this subject. Yet in all the versions of this period, the Magi kneel before the Madonna exactly as a worshiper would kneel before an altar. In these panels, therefore, the table cannot be the only allusion to the altar.

The statuesque Virgin in Rogier's painting, like similar figures in the other Adorations of this period, acts as Christ's throne. She supports him on a white cloth on her platform-like lap, like the enthroned Virgins by Van Eyck considered above (cf. Figs. 6 and 9–11). Her rectilinearity recalls, therefore, the Eyckian analogy between Mary and the altar.

Other details in Rogier's panel substantiate this interpretation. If the table to Mary's right functions as an altar, as Nilgen has suggested, it must also refer to the "living altar" of Christ, the Virgin herself. The sarcophagus-like manger directly behind the table alludes to the interpretation of the altar as both manger and tomb. Finally, the tiny crucifix on the post behind the Virgin hangs almost directly above her, as crucifixes frequently hung above the lay altar. Whereas this detail can be interpreted as a simple allusion to Christ's inevitable sacrifice, it is also logical as one of the clarifying features of the analogy between the Virgin and the altar.

This crucifix may also identify the structure behind Mary as a church. Scholars usually interpret the crumbling edifices in Nativities and Adorations of this period as references to the synagogue that began to decay with the birth of Christ.[70] In this case, however, Rogier may have intended to refer to the newly erected Church instead, since a crucifix would obviously be totally out of place in any part of a synagogue.

A dramatic variation of Rogier's panel by Memling in Madrid (Figs. 41 and 48) lends support to this possibility. Here again, the Adoration of the Magi occupies the central position in a triptych devoted to Infancy themes. In this panel, Memling moved the Virgin closer to the center of the scene and transformed the pillar that appears in Rogier's panel into a column, to which she seems almost attached. No crucifix adorns the column, but there can be no question that the structure to which it belongs is meant to be a church. Its semicircular projection behind Mary ingeniously evokes the idea of a rounded apse.[71] As in Jan's *Madonna of Canon van der Paele* (Fig. 10), the central Virgin in front of this structure appears exactly where one would expect to find the altar in an apse. A tomb-like manger and a triangular table on either side of Mary also allude to the altar. As in the Eyckian paintings that we considered in Chapter I, Memling's statuesque Virgin functions as the altar-table, the *mensa panis vitae,* in the central place of honor.

The Virgin-altar analogy recurs frequently in Adorations of this period. A particularly lucid example of it occurs in Gerard David's panel in London (Fig. 42).[72] Here, Mary sits on the edge of a sarcophagus-shaped manger, with her drapery cascading over it. Instead of kissing the Infant's hand or foot, as in Rogier's and Memling's versions, respectively, the first king kneels in prayer before him. David's rectilinear Virgin recalls Mary's form in the Rolin *Madonna* by Van Eyck (Fig. 11), where the chancellor also kneels in reverence. In this example, therefore, David again echoes the Eyckian comparison between the Virgin and the altar.

The Rolin *Madonna* seems to have inspired a painting by Bosch as well. In the center panel of his Prado *Epiphany* (Fig. 43), the statuesque Virgin again recalls the throne-like figure in Jan's painting.[73] Here, Bosch expanded the Eucharistic associations of the Virgin-altar analogy through the first king's gift, prominently placed at Mary's feet. This gift, a statuette of the sacrifice of Isaac, prefigures Christ's coming sacrifice; the visual sources of this subject as a prototype of the Eucharistic rite can be traced back to the early Christian period.[74] The sacramental intent of Bosch's triptych is clarified by the *Mass of Saint Gregory* on its exterior wings (Fig.

42. Gerard David, *Adoration of the Magi,* 23⅜ x 23″ (59.5 x 58.5 cm). London, The National Gallery.

43. Hieronymus Bosch, *Epiphany* Triptych, interior, 54⅜ x 54⅜″ (138 x 138 cm). Madrid, Museo del Prado.

44. Hieronymus Bosch, *Epiphany* Triptych, exterior: *Mass of Saint Gregory,* 54⅜ x 26″ (138 x 66 cm.) Madrid, Museo del Prado.

44). The miraculous transformation of the Host into the body of Christ in this scene leads directly to the dramatization of the analogy between the Incarnation and the Transubstantiation that appears on the interior.[75] No table is necessary here, because Mary, as the altar, holds the sacred body that is at once the object of the kings' worship and the pictorial parallel of the substance of the Eucharist.

As in Bosch's triptych, Rogier's Columba Altarpiece focuses on a central Adoration of the Magi that stresses the Eucharistic implications of the theme. In Rogier's work, however, the scenes on the wings expand this meaning. We have already considered the *Annunciation* on the left panel, which presents the miracle of the Incarnation in a space that is both a bedroom and a sanctuary. Similar sacramental associations also appear in the *Presentation in the Temple* on the right wing (Fig. 45), where the connections with the sacrifice of the Mass are perhaps the most dramatic of all.

In Rogier's *Presentation,* the scene is a Romanesque church interior. In the foreground of this sacred space, Mary presents the Infant to Simeon over an altar. Any realistic rendering of this theme must obviously portray it in an ecclesiastical setting. Like the other early Netherlandish Presentations, however, Rogier's panel deliberately stresses the Eucharistic meaning of the subject, for it portrays the Christ Child above the altar as a parallel to the sacrificial Host.

In his account of the Presentation, Luke relates that Mary and Joseph brought the Christ Child to the temple in Jerusalem forty days after his birth, as prescribed by Jewish law, and presented him to the Lord along with a sacrifice of two turtledoves, or young pigeons (Luke 2:22–39). This description actually combines two Jewish customs: the purification of the mother forty days after the birth of a male child and the redemption of the firstborn for five shekels thirty days after his birth.[76] According to Luke, Simeon was not a priest, but an old man who could not die until he had seen the Lord. When the Holy Family entered the temple, Simeon received the Child and recited the words that were to form one of the major canticles of the liturgy, the *Nunc Dimittis.* An old prophetess, Anna, is the only other participant in Luke's account.

As in the other two panels of his triptych, Rogier did not rely entirely on the Biblical passage for inspiration, for his *Presentation* includes several unidentified figures as well as the participants in Luke's account. Joseph holds a burning candle behind the Virgin, who mounts the steps of the altar to present her offering. In some of its details, in fact, Rogier's

45. Rogier van der Weyden, Columba Altarpiece, right wing: *Presentation in the Temple,* 54⅜ x 27½″ (138 x 70 cm). Munich, Alte Pinakothek.

46. Jacques Daret, *Presentation in the Temple*, 22½ x 20½" (57 x 52 cm). Paris, Musée du Petit Palais.

scene seems closer to the liturgical celebration of the Feast of the Presentation than to the passage in the Gospels.

From the fifth century on, the Presentation of Christ in the Temple was commemorated in the liturgy on February 2 at Candlemas, which also celebrates the Purification of the Virgin.[77] Traditional ceremonies on this day included the recitation of the *Nunc Dimittis* and a procession with lighted candles, which gave the feast its name.[78] Later in the Middle Ages, dramatic ceremonies at Candlemas expanded this procession to include figures impersonating Joseph, Simeon, and the Virgin, who presented an effigy of the Christ Child at the high altar.[79]

The candle that Joseph holds in Rogier's panel may allude to the Candlemas ceremonies.[80] This reference is even more prominent in Jacques Daret's version of the theme in Paris (Fig. 46), where four of the seven figures surrounding the altar hold similar candles.[81] In Rogier's panel, moreover, the beginning words of Simeon's canticle are inscribed above Christ's head; although this canticle comes directly from Luke's Gospel (Luke 2:29–32), it was also recited in the Candlemas ceremony.

Even more relevant for our purposes, perhaps, is the way Mary holds the Infant directly above the altar in both versions. The body of Christ in these scenes appears in the very place that is occupied by the sacrificial Host during Mass. Daret's panel, in fact, includes additional references to the ultimate sacrifice, for its stained glass windows portray the story of one of the traditional prototypes of Christ's death and Resurrection, Noah.[82]

If the Infant parallels the Host in these scenes, then the figure who presents him at the altar must function as the celebrant who offers the Eucharist on behalf of the congregation. Yet, in both of these panels, it is the Virgin who performs the oblation.

The question of Mary's priesthood is highly controversial.[83] Medieval writers often praised her sacrifice at the altar during the Presentation in the Temple, but they did not specifically describe her as a priest. Her function as the celebrant seems intentionally strong, however, in one of Saint Bernard's sermons on the Purification: "Offer your son, sacred Virgin, and present the blessed fruit of your womb to God. For the reconciliation of us all, offer the holy Host [which is] pleasing to God."[84] Ludolphus of Saxony quoted Saint Bernard's words in his own discussion of the Presentation, in his widely read *Vita Christi.*[85]

An unusually explicit French panel of 1437 at the Louvre (Fig. 47)[86] illustrates that the concept of the Virgin's priesthood still existed in northern European thought in the first half of the fifteenth century. *Le Sacerdoce de la Vierge* belongs to a series of paintings of the Virgin commissioned annually for the Cathedral of Amiens.[87] It depicts Mary in the garb of the high priest of the Old Testament, as described in Exodus 28:1–35.[88] The liturgically vested Virgin prefigures the New Testament priest, Christ, just as the figures of Abel, Abraham, and Melchizedek on the altarpiece behind her foreshadow his inevitable sacrifice. She holds the hand of the youthful Christ as if to encourage his participation in the Mass, in the nave of a church that may portray Amiens Cathedral itself.[89]

Like Rogier's Columba *Presentation,* this painting depicts the Virgin before an altar in an ecclesiastical setting. Mary's costume identifies her as a priest, but she does not enact the sacrifice. In Rogier's scene, on the other hand, she wears no liturgical vestments, but it is she who elevates the body of the Infant over the altar. She acts here as the sacrificing priest, who presents a visual parallel of the daily offering at Mass.

The Eucharistic implications of the Presentation make it a fitting climax to the story of Christ's childhood. The Feast of Candlemas to which it relates, moreover, concludes the Christmas cycle in the liturgical year.[90] By including the Presentation in the Temple as the final scene of his triptych, therefore, Rogier depicted both the ceremony that served as the climax to the annual celebration of Christ's birth and a dramatization of the sacrificial rite performed at the altar.

In Memling's adaptation of the Columba Altarpiece at the Prado (Fig. 48), the center and right panels echo Rogier's subjects; on the left wing,

47. *Le Sacerdoce de la Vierge,* 39⅜ x 23⅝″ (100 x 60 cm). Paris, Musée du Louvre.

however, the Nativity replaces the Annunciation.[91] This substitution may have resulted from a desire to parallel the ceremonies of the Christmas season. The arrangement of the subjects in this triptych, in fact, corresponds to the order of the three major feasts of Christ's Infancy in the church year: Christmas, Epiphany, and Candlemas.

As in the case of Rogier's altarpiece, however, Memling's triptych would have been suitable for use in the daily Mass as well as on these special feast days. We have already considered the sacramental implications of its central *Adoration.* The two side panels certainly continue the Eucharistic associations of the Nativity and Presentation in the Temple that we have studied in other versions of the period. Memling's emphasis on the body of Christ in each of the three scenes, moreover, can hardly be coincidental. The careful placement of the Infant in each panel may even contribute to the general meaning of the altarpiece. In Memling's trip-

48. Hans Memling, Altarpiece of the Adoration of the Magi, 37⅞ x 106⅝″ (95 x 271 cm). Madrid, Museo del Prado.

tych, the Infant progresses from a prone position on the ground in the *Nativity* at the left to a seated posture on the altar-like lap of the Virgin in the central *Adoration*. The final uplifting of the Child in the *Presentation* at the right concludes a gradual rise of his body that evokes the idea of the elevation of the Host.[92]

In this triptych, therefore, Memling deliberately interpreted the Incarnation subjects in relation to the daily miracle of Transubstantiation. As in the other Infancy panels we have considered in this chapter, his altarpiece dramatizes the meaning of the Eucharistic rite as well as the Christmas rituals.

NOTES TO CHAPTER II

1. Hirn, 474. The word "overshadow" occurs in Luke's description of the Annunciation, where it does not have the modern connotation of superiority.

2. Katzenellenbogen, 12ff.

3. Nilgen, 311f., especially nn. 3–11. This study is one of the basic treatments of the Eucharistic implications of Infancy themes. See also Philip, 93f.; Gottlieb, 74; and Purtle, 11ff.

4. I.e., in the Broederlam Altarpiece in the Musée des Beaux-Arts in Dijon; for this work, see especially Panofsky, 86ff. and 131ff.

5. For this altarpiece, preserved in the Cloisters Collection of the Metropolitan Museum of Art and usually dated about 1427–28, see especially Friedländer, II, #54; Panofsky, 164ff.; Minott, 267ff.; and Davies, 258ff. In addition to the bibliography cited by Davies, see L. Campbell, "Robert Campin, the Master of Flémalle, and the Master of Mérode," *Burlington Magazine,* CXVI, 1974, 634ff., where the author reviews the problem of the attribution of the altarpiece. For a recent attempt to minimize the symbolism of this work, see J. de Coo, "A Medieval Look at the Merode Annunciation," *Zeitschrift für Kunstgeschichte,* XLIV, 1981, 114ff.

6. Ch. IV; Ragusa and Green, 16. See *ibid.,* xxi f., for the date, problematic authorship, and diffusion of this frequently translated text, which will be used here to exemplify the popular treatises of this type.

7. See especially Philip, 94, and Gottlieb, 65ff.

8. Gottlieb, 65ff. Cf. above, Ch. I, nn. 13–14 and the accompanying text.

9. University Library, ms. 400, fol. 1; Philip, fig. 97. For this manuscript, see also Delaissé, 41, fig. 86.

10. *Rationale Divinorum Officiorum,* Book I, ch. 1, 39 (Barthélemy, 27f. and Neale and Webb, 27), quoted in Gottlieb, 67. See Hirn, 102ff., for the reasons that necessitated the washing of the priest's hands before and after Mass.

11. Both Philip, 92. cf. and Gottlieb, "'En ipse stat post parietem nostrum,'" 79, recognized the niche in the Ghent *Annunciation* as a *piscina.*

12. Philip, 94, n. 192. Cf. Gottlieb, 73, where it is suggested that the sixteen sides of the table refer to the sixteen prophets and, therefore, indicate that the table is still a Hebrew altar. For Nilgen's interpretation of the table in Epiphany scenes, see below, Ch. I1, n. 69 and the accompanying text.

13. Gottlieb, 74f.

14. *Ibid.,* 74. For this manner of tying the stole, see *Oxford Dictionary,* 1312. McNamee first characterized the liturgical garments of angels in this period, in "Further Symbolism," 142f. He later expanded his ideas in a fundamental study, "Origin of the Vested Angel," 263ff.

15. Westfälisches Landesmuseum für Kunst und Kulturgeschichte, Ms. 530, fol. 16v. For this manuscript, see especially P. Pieper, "Das Stundenbuch der Katharina van Lochorst und der Meister der Katharina von Kleve," *Westfalen,* XLIV, 1966, 97ff., with the date of c. 1450 given on 127.

16. E.g., the two miniatures of the Crucifixion and the Descent in the *Hours of Catherine of Cleves* (New York, Pierpont Morgan Library, M. 945, fol. 66v. and 69v.), which derive from Campin's *Descent* Triptych; see Panofsky, 176. For these miniatures, see J.

Plummer, *The Hours of Catherine of Cleves,* New York, 1966, #26 and 28.

17. Pieper, "Stundenbuch," 157.

18. Cf. McNamee, "Further Symbolism," 142 and n. 3, and "Origin of the Vested Angel," 276.

19. For Annunciations in church interiors, see especially Robb, 480ff., and Purtle, 40ff.

20. National Gallery of Art; Friedländer, I, pl. 57. For an intensive investigation of this panel, see Purtle, Ch. 3, 40ff. A previously unrecorded version in a church, which bears Petrus Christus' signature, was recently acquired by the Groeninge Museum in Bruges.

21. Panofsky, 138f., has suggested that the progression from Romanesque architecture in the upper stories to the Gothic style at ground level signifies the transition from the Old to the New Law that occurs at Christ's Incarnation. But cf. the recent comparison of this interior to Saint-Quentin in Tournai by T. W. Lyman, "Architectural Portraiture and Jan van Eyck's Washington Annunciation," *Gesta,* XX/1, 1981, 263ff.

22. Friedländer, II, #9 and 49. For the triptych of which the Louvre version was the center panel, see especially Davies, 236f. See pp. 60–71 of this chapter for the Columba Altarpiece, preserved in the Alte Pinakothek.

23. Two versions of this composition survive, and both probably derive from an original by Campin. For the panel reproduced here, see below, Ch. IV, n. 88 and the accompanying text. For the other version, see Friedländer, II, #73a.

24. A barrel vault also appears in Bouts's *Annunciation* at the Prado (*ibid.,* III, #1).

25. For the popularity of this play, see Young, II, 246.

26. *Ibid.,* 246.

27. *Ibid.,* 246 and 480ff. See also the sixteenth-century text from Bruges, described in Purtle, 47ff., and reprinted there on 193ff.

28. McNamee, "Drama," 37ff., fig. 1. For the influence of this ceremony on Flemish painting, see his discussion in "Origin of the Vested Angel," 276. For the Aix *Annunciation,* see also Ring, 204, #91.

29. Purtle, 46ff.

30. Similar sculptural doves appear, e.g., in Christus' *Annunciation* in Berlin (Friedländer, I, pl. 77), in Hugo's exterior wings of the Portinari Altarpiece at the Uffizi (*ibid.,* IV, #10), and in Memling's *Annunciation* in the Lehman Collection at the Metropolitan Museum in New York (*ibid.,* VIa, #26).

31. See, e.g., the work at the Metropolitan Museum, reproduced in Philip, fig. 64, with a discussion on 69. For Eucharistic doves in general, see Hirn, 114f.; Raible, 143ff.; Braun, II, 608ff. and pl. 353–55; and Maffei, 29ff., fig. 4.

32. I.e., the Wednesday after December 13; cf. Young, II, 246, and Purtle, 46.

33. Staatliche Museen; Friedländer, IV, #15. For this painting, in addition to the bibliography cited in Lane, "'Ecce Panis Angelorum,'" nn. 1–4, see Thompson and Campbell, 90f., where the authors agree with the late dating of c. 1480 accepted by most scholars.

34. Ch. VII: Ragusa and Green, 38.

35. For St. Brigitta's text of c. 1370 (*Revelationes,* VII, 21, and 22) and a translation of it, see Cornell, *Iconography,* 9ff. For discussions of its influence on fifteenth-century Nativities, see especially *ibid.,* 13ff.; Panofsky, 46; Schiller, I, 88ff.; and Upton, "Devotional Imagery," 59ff. See also Fig. 36 here for an example of the Virgin reclining at the Nativity.

36. This discussion of Hugo's painting is based on Lane, "'Ecce Panis Angelorum,'" passim.

37. For the house-altarpiece of c. 1370, in the Bayerisches Nationalmuseum, to which this panel belongs, see Stange, II, 99f., fig. 124, and the bibliography cited in Lane, "'Ecce Panis Angelorum,'" n. 11.

38. *Expositio in Evangelium Lucae* (Migne, *P.L.,* CXIV, 896C): ". . . positus in praesepio, id est corpus Christi super altare. . . ." Cf. Katzenellenbogen, 108, n. 23. For additional sources, which begin in the early Christian period, see Nilgen, 311, nn. 4–6, and Sinanoglou, 494f., nn. 15–18.

39. Gregory, *Liber Sacramentorum, In Die Natalis Domini* (Migne, *P.L.,* LXXVIII, 31D): "Et qui eum qui Panis est angelorum in praesepi Ecclesiae cibum fecit esse fidelium animalium . . . ." Cf. Lane, "'Ecce Panis Angelorum,'" n. 18, for other connections with the liturgy.

40. For the various versions of this type of Host miracle, see Browe, *Eucharistischen Wunder,* 100ff.; Sinanoglou, 491ff; and Lane, "'Ecce Panis Angelorum,'" 479, nn. 20–24 (figs. 5–6) and the accompanying text.

41. *Homilia VIII, In Die Natalis Domini* (Migne, *P.L.,* LXXVI, 1104A): "Qui bene etiam in Bethlehem nascitur: Bethlehem quippe domus panis interpretatur." Cf. Panofsky, 333 and 333[4] and Katzenellenbogen, 12 and 108, n. 21.

42. Florence, Uffizi (Friedländer, IV, #10). For the Eucharistic intent of this

scene, see especially McNamee, "Further Symbolism," 142. Cf. Panofsky, 333f.; Koch, 76 and n. 49; Nilgen, 316, n. 45; and Philip, 216.

43. Metropolitan Museum of Art; Friedländer, VIb, #160. Cf. Lane, "'Ecce Panis Angelorum,'" 485, fig. 16. This motif also occurs in scenes of the Adoration of the Magi: e.g., in David's panel in Munich (Friedländer, VIb, #181).

44. This function of the curtains was explained by Durandus, *Rationale,* Book I, ch. iii, 35 (Barthélemy, 57f., and Neale and Webb, 61f.). For the prevalence of altar curtains in northern Europe in the late Gothic period, see Braun, II, 133ff. See also above, Ch. I, nn. 34–35 and the accompanying text.

45. For the opening of the curtains, see especially Pugin, 107f. and 237f.; Hirn, 114 and 500, n. 7; Braun, II, 167; and Jungmann, II, 140 and 140, n. 11.

46. For the authenticity of the liturgical objects in this picture, preserved in the National Gallery, see Davies, *Early Netherlandish School,* 109ff., where the author has attributed it to a Netherlandish-trained artist who worked in Paris. For another illustration of altar curtains, see Fig. 43 here.

47. Cf. Katzenellenbogen, 12ff. For this window, see Y. Delaporte, *Les Vitraux de la cathédrale de Chartres,* Chartres, 1926, 149 f., pl. vol. I, pl. IV. For other examples, see Lane, "'Ecce Panis Angelorum,'" figs. 9–10.

48. Young, II, 19. For the Shepherds' Play in general, see *ibid.,* 4ff.; Young, "Officium Pastorum," 299ff.; and Hardison, 223f. (for the problem of dating).

49. See the sources cited in Lane, "'Ecce Panis Angelorum,'" n. 3.

50. Young, II, 190, and Hardison, 254. For the Play of the Prophets in general, see Young, II, 125ff., and Young, "Ordo Prophetarum," 1ff.

51. Young, II, 126. Cf. McNamee, "Drama," 38.

52. For the parallels between Jeremiah and Christ, see Lane, "'Ecce Panis Angelorum,'" 484 and nn. 62–64.

53. This was suggested by Held in his review of Panofsky's book, 232. For an example of this type of tomb, see Nino Pisano's Tomb of Archbishop Simone Saltorelli, in S. Caterina, Pisa (E. Panofsky, *Tomb Sculpture,* New York, 1964, fig. 336). See also the examples reproduced in *ibid.,* figs. 333 and 397–98.

54. *Historia Ecclesiastica et Mystica Contemplatio* (Migne, *P.G.,* XCVIII, 390B): "Altare est et dicitur praesepe et sepul-

chrum Domini. . . ." Cf. Young, II, 8, and Katzenellenbogen, 108, n. 23.

55. Young, II, 8. For the *Visitatio Sepulchri,* or *Quem Queritis* play, see especially *ibid.,* I, 239ff.; and Hardison, 178ff.; see also below, Ch. III, n. 56 and the accompanying text. The *Officium Pastorum* begins, "Quem queritis in presepe . . ."; these words echo the opening words of the angel in the *Visitatio Sepulchri:* "Quem queritis in sepulchro."

56. National Gallery of Art; Friedländer, I, pl. 102. Upton, 193ff., first recognized the sacramental nature of this painting, which is usually dated c. 1445; he expanded his ideas in "Devotional Imagery," 49ff.

57. *Ibid.,* 65.

58. *Ibid.,* 72, where Joseph is metaphorically associated with Moses.

59. Cf. *Ibid.,* 68 and n. 45. For the closely related panel of the Nativity by Bouts at the Prado, see Friedländer, III, #1. Hirn, 94f., discusses the need to protect the altar from dust as the origin of the ciborium.

60. National Gallery; Friedländer, V, #1. For this painting, see especially Snyder, 124f., and Davies, *Early Netherlandish School,* 57f.

61. For this triptych, in the Alte Pinakothek, whose name derives from the fact that it was in a chapel in St. Columba in Cologne, see Friedländer, II, #49, and Davies, 227f. For arguments dating it in the first half of the 1450s rather than late in Rogier's career, as scholars usually do, see A. Markham Schulz, "The Columba Altarpiece and Roger van der Weyden's Stylistic Development," *Münchner Jahrbuch der Bildenden Kunst,* XXII, 1971, 63ff.

62. See above, Ch. 2, n. 22 and the accompanying text.

63. Ch. IX; Ragusa and Green, 50f. Cf. the passage in the *Golden Legend* (Voragine, 87).

64. For the Offertory rite, see especially *Oxford Dictionary,* 994, and Jungmann, II, 1ff.

65. Nilgen, 313, and Von Simson, *Sacred Fortress,* 29ff. and 94f., discuss the relationship of these mosaics to the Offertory rite. See also Young, II, 33f., for references to the story of the Three Kings in early Offertory rites.

66. See the convenient chart of the chronology of the plays in Hardison, 314, where the page numbers refer to the texts printed in Young, II, 34ff. Cf. above, Ch. I, nn. 36–39 and the accompanying text.

67. Nilgen, 312f., and Forsyth, *Throne,*

56. Young, II, 47, has suggested that the *Officium Stellae* derived from the Shepherds' Play, where the inclusion of midwives is somewhat more logical.

68. McNamee, "Additional Eucharistic Allusion," 109.

69. Nilgen, 315f.

70. E.g., Panofsky, 135ff.

71. Cf. Nilgen, 316, and Hull, 113. For this painting, preserved at the Museo del Prado, see below, Ch. II, nn. 91–92 and the accompanying text.

72. National Gallery; Friedländer, VIb, #182.

73. Tolnay, 43, first noted this resemblance; cf. Philip, 217f., and Gibson, 112. For the Prado *Epiphany,* see Friedländer, V. #68.

74. E.g., in the sixth-century mosaic in San Vitale in Ravenna (F. W. Deichmann, *Frühchristliche Bauten und Mosaiken von Ravenna,* Wiesbaden, 1958, pl. 327). See E. Lucchesi Palli, "Abraham," in *Lexikon,* I, 23ff., for other examples and bibliography for this typology.

75. Tolnay, 43f., first described the sacramental implications of the Prado *Epiphany.* Cf. Philip, "Prado Epiphany," 280ff.; Gibson, 112; and Harbison, 69f. For the Mass of St. Gregory, see below, Ch. IV, nn. 87–88 and the accompanying text.

76. This combination of events was recognized by Shorr, 17ff., in the most comprehensive study of the theme, where earlier versions of it are illustrated.

77. *Ibid.,* 19.

78. For Candlemas, see especially *Oxford Dictionary,* 229.

79. Young, "Dramatic Ceremonies," 100ff., and Young, II, 250ff.

80. Cf. Mâle, *Religious Art,* 127f., where it is suggested that the candles in twelfth-century Presentations derive from Candlemas ceremonies.

81. Petit Palais; Friedländer, II, #80. An even more elaborate reference to Candlemas occurs in Stephan Lochner's *Presentation in the Temple* in Darmstadt (Hessisches Landesmuseum), where a crowd of choir boys hold candles in the foreground. For the Eucharistic implications of this German panel, in which the Infant sits on the altar, see L. Brand (Philip), *Stephan Lochners Hochaltar von St. Katharinen zu Köln,* Hamburg, 1938, 50ff., with the painting reproduced as the frontispiece.

82. For the identification of these scenes and the recognition of their sacrificial content, see G. Smith, "The Betrothal of the Virgin by the Master of Flémalle," *Pantheon,* XXX, 1972, 132, n. 64. For the use of the story of Noah as a prefiguration of Christ's sacrifice, see R. Daut, "Noe (Noah)," in *Lexikon,* IV, 619.

83. For the problem of whether or not Mary can be considered a priest, see especially the comprehensive study by Laurentin, passim.

84. *De Purificatione B. Mariae Sermo III,* 2 (Migne, *P.L.,* CLXXXIII, 370C): "Offer filium tuum, Virgo sacrata, et benedictum fructum ventris tui Domino repraesenta. Offer ad nostram omnium reconciliationem hostiam sanctam, Deo placentem." This passage is quoted in Laurentin, 142.

85. Part I, Ch. XII: *De Praesentatione Domini in Templum* (Ludolphus, I, 107).

86. For this painting, see especially Dupont, 265ff., and Ring, 218, #158.

87. Dupont, 271. For the Puy d'Amiens, see also G. Durand, *Tableaux et chants royaux de la confrérie du Puy Notre Dame d'Amiens,* Amiens and Paris, 1911.

88. Cf. Ring, 218, where Mary is described as a "priest officiating the first Mass," and Purtle, 12 and 12, n. 32. Laurentin, "Digne vesture," 258f., identifies the costume, but denies that Mary actually functions as a priest in this panel.

89. Dupont, 270. For the suggestion that Mary is portrayed as a priest in Van Eyck's Berlin *Madonna in a Church,* on which this painting may be based, see Purtle, 153.

90. C. Smith, "Candlemas," *New Catholic Encyclopedia,* III, 1967, 23.

91. Friedländer, VIa, #1. Cf. the similar Floreins Altarpiece, in the Hospital of St. John in Bruges (*ibid.,* VIa, #2), which is signed and dated 1479. The advanced space of the Prado version suggests a later date than is usually accepted; see Lane, *Memling,* 74 and #61.

92. A similar progression occurs in the Floreins Altarpiece. Cf. Hull, 119, where the author has mentioned the concentration on the Christ Child in the Prado version.

49. Rogier van der Weyden, *Crucifixion* Triptych, 43¾ x 55½" (110 x 141 cm). Vienna, Kunsthistorisches Museum.

III
The Eucharistic Rite
and the Easter Liturgy

When the priest enacts the sacrament of the Eucharist at the altar, he makes an offering that, according to Catholic dogma, repeats the sacrifice of Christ on the cross. The priest's authority for presenting this offering, or oblation, comes from the Church, on whose behalf he has been ordained to perform the ceremony. During every Mass, therefore, the Church, in the person of the priest, reenacts the sacrifice that occurred for the redemption of mankind.[1]

Any scene from Christ's Passion can be used to explain the meaning of the daily oblation to the worshiper. The later events of the story, from the Crucifixion to the Entombment, however, relate more clearly to the sacrificial rite than subjects such as the Entry into Jerusalem or the Flagellation. In early Netherlandish painting, the later events appear almost exclusively. Most of the preserved interpretations of these subjects in this period, moreover, neglect the historical details of the themes in order to stress their sacramental implications.

Early Netherlandish Passion scenes dramatize the meaning of the Eucharistic sacrifice. They stress the role of the Church in the presentation of the daily oblation. As in the Infancy scenes that we considered in the previous chapter, these panels also depict parallels for other liturgical ceremonies performed at the altar. In this case, however, they relate to the rituals of Easter rather than Christmas.

As discussed in the previous chapter, the miraculous Transformation of the Host into the body of Christ occurs during the Transubstantiation. No matter how strong the worshiper's faith may be, however, what he actually sees when he looks at the consecrated Host is still a wafer of bread. If his eyes were to move to a nearby image in which Christ's sacrifice was more explicit, therefore, he would not have to strain to see it in his imagination.

In early Netherlandish painting, the Passion scenes portray dramatic visual explanations of the rites that the faithful witnessed at the altar. The emphasis on the Eucharistic associations of their subjects is the focus of this chapter.

Rogier van der Weyden's Crucifixion *Triptych*

Early Netherlandish Crucifixions usually depict only the essential details of the actual event. Frequently, they include anachronistic figures or settings that negate their historical tenor. In Rogier's *Crucifixion* Triptych in Vienna (Fig. 49),[2] for instance, a luxuriant landscape behind the foreground figures bears no trace of the thieves who were crucified along with Christ or the Roman soldiers who tormented him. At Christ's feet, the Virgin drops to her knees to embrace the Cross as passionately as if it were Christ himself, while two fifteenth-century worshipers kneel in reverence beside her.

The story of the Crucifixion appears in each of the four Gospels, in long passages filled with narrative detail.[3] In one of the most emotional chapters of the *Meditations on the Life of Christ,* moreover, these accounts are elaborated still further.[4] Yet Rogier's interpretation of the subject reveals no attempt to echo the details of these written sources.

Comparison of the Vienna *Crucifixion* Triptych with earlier, more narrative versions of the theme clarifies its extraordinary originality. In a grisaille silk chapel hanging produced in Paris about 1375, the so-called *Parement de Narbonne* (Fig. 50), for instance, the numerous witnesses of the event divide into two groups at the foot of the central cross.[5] The two thieves hang on their crosses on either side of Christ. Below them, the suffering women mentioned in the Gospel accounts huddle in the left foreground, with Christ's tormentors crowding in from both sides. The worshiping King Charles V and Queen Jeanne de Bourbon flank the scene in compartments that clearly separate them from the main action.

Rogier's painting is far less crowded than the scene in the *Parement de Narbonne.* It portrays only six figures accompanying Christ in the foreground of a peaceful landscape, which stretches across all three panels of the triptych. Mary Magdalen and Saint Veronica stand quietly in the wings. Four angels hover overhead, adding to the perfect balance of the composition. In the center, John the Evangelist reaches out to support the Virgin, who clings to the foot of the cross in an agonizing expression of grief. Christ's loincloth flutters gracefully in a nonexistent breeze. The only other figures are the unidentified donor and his wife, who kneel anachronously in the space of the Biblical scene.

The *Crucifixion* Triptych portrays a nonhistorical, sacramental image.

50. *Parement de Narbonne,* center section: *Crucifixion,* height 30¾″ (78 cm). Paris, Musée du Louvre.

Its message is just as timeless as more traditional Gothic examples of the subject, such as the *Calvary of Hendrijk van Rijn* of 1363 (Fig. 51). In this painting, which is one of the few preserved Netherlandish panels of the fourteenth century, a supplicant also kneels at the foot of the cross. An inscription identifies him, describes his donation of the picture to the Church of Saint John in Utrecht, and asks the viewer to pray for him.[6] The patternized gold background defines the celestial space of the picture and removes it totally from the earthly world of the observer. Hendrijk van Rijn can kneel below the cross here, in almost the same scale as the holy figures, because the picture portrays the meaning of the daily oblation that he has witnessed at the altar rather than Christ's historical sacrifice.[7]

Rogier's painting may look more realistic than this early panel, but it is just as clearly intended to emphasize the sacramental nature of the theme. The sweeping landscape that replaces the traditional gold ground serves merely as a backdrop for the sacred image in the foreground. In this triptych, the full-size supplicants can appear in the same space as the holy figures precisely because the scene is nonhistorical. These pious worship-

51. *Calvary of Hendrijk van Rijn,* 52⅜ x 51¼″ (133 x 130 cm). Antwerp, Koninklijk Museum.

ers pray before an illustration of the sacrifice that they saw performed during their own lifetime, at every Mass.

Rogier's triptych is, like all of his Crucifixions, a dramatic visual explanation of the meaning of the Eucharistic rite. Consideration of another of his interpretations of this theme may help to clarify it in the Vienna altarpiece.

In the central panel of Rogier's Altarpiece of the Seven Sacraments in Antwerp (Fig. 52), Christ's cross fills almost the entire height of the nave

52. Rogier van der Weyden, Altarpiece of the Seven Sacraments, 78¾ x 87¾" (200 x 223 cm). Antwerp, Koninklijk Museum.

53. Rogier van der Weyden, Altarpiece of the Seven Sacraments, detail of Figure 52.

of a Gothic cathedral.[8] Directly behind this enormous apparition, at an altar in front of the choir screen, a priest raises the Eucharistic wafer in the ceremony of Transubstantiation (Fig. 53). Christ, raised high on his cross, illustrates the meaning of the elevated Host.

The crucified Christ appears often in earlier illustrations of the Eucharistic rite. Visual sources for this tradition occur in early medieval illumination, when the "T" of "Te igitur" at the beginning of the Canon of the Mass is transformed into Christ's cross.[9] In later examples, a priest sometimes stands at an altar that is adorned with a crucifix: for example, in the early-fifteenth-century Dutch *Tafel van der Kersten Ghelove* by Dirc van Delft in New York (Fig. 54).[10] In the miniature on folio 38v. of this manu-

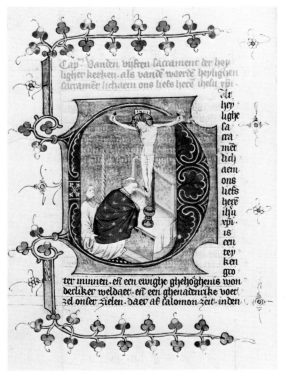

Within the illuminated initial, the following text appears:

Cap. Vanden vijfften sacrament der hey
ligher kerken. als vande waerde heylighen
sacramět lichaem ons liefs here ihesu xpi.

Dat
hey
lighe
sa
cra
mět
lich
aem
ons
liefs
here
ihu
xpi.
is
een
tey
ken
groo

ter minnen. en een ewighe ghehoghenis won
derliker weldaet. en een ghenadenlike voet
sel onser zielen. daer af salomon zeit. inden

54. *Sacrament of the Eucharist,*
Dirc van Delft, *Tafel van der*
Kersten Ghelove, 8⅝ x 6⅛"
(21.9 x 15.5 cm). New York,
Pierpont Morgan Library.

script, blood pours out of Christ's wounds into the chalice below, where it is transformed into the wine of the Eucharist.

No crucifix appears above the altar in the Altarpiece of the Seven Sacraments. Instead, Rogier depicted a gigantic Crucifixion with the Virgin, Saint John, and the three Maries, all anachronously contained within a Gothic basilica. The crucified Christ dominates the entire altarpiece. Rogier's incongruous placement of the cross in a church, directly in front of the elevation of the Host, explains the meaning of the Eucharistic rite as clearly as does the Dutch miniature.[11]

The Vienna *Crucifixion* Triptych does not portray the scene in a church, but its sacramental message is equally explicit. It differs from all of the examples mentioned thus far in its inclusion of an intimate motif that arouses the sympathy of the beholder. With tears streaming down her face, the Virgin desperately embraces the cross in an intensely realistic portrayal of a mother who has just lost her only son. This action contrasts dramatically with Mary's traditional fainting posture in Crucifixions of the late Middle Ages (for example, in Figs. 50 and 52). Although the Magdalen sometimes grasps the cross in other versions of the scene,[12] there is no precedent for the Virgin's position in Rogier's painting.

Scholars have recognized how unusual Mary's action is in this triptych, but they have not adequately explained the reasons for it.[13] In the Middle Ages, writers compared the Virgin's emotional suffering at the Crucifixion to Christ's physical pain. They spoke of her intense sorrow, or "compassion," as a parallel to the Passion itself. The idea that this "compassion" allowed Mary to be a co-redeemer of mankind has its sources in the twelfth century, but only in the fifteenth century did it reach its height in popularity as a devotional theme.[14]

In a fundamental study some years ago, Von Simson interpreted the parallel positions of the fainting Virgin and the dead Christ in Rogier's *Descent from the Cross* (Fig. 56) as a literal interpretation of Mary's role as co-redeemer.[15] This theme is perhaps even more emphatic in the Vienna *Crucifixion,* where the still conscious Virgin actively displays her grief. Yet here, and, as we shall see presently, in Rogier's *Descent from the Cross* as well, Mary's suffering also has a wider implication.

As early as the time of the Church fathers, the sacrament of the Eucharist was understood to include the self-oblation of the Church, which Mary symbolizes.[16] Later theologians also compared the Virgin's suffering to the sacrifice of the Mass. Johann Tauler (d. 1361), for instance, described Mary's offering on Calvary as follows:

> As the heavenly Father offered his only Son, the living Host, on the altar of the cross, and still offers him daily in the sacrament for the salvation of men, so that he might be the perpetual intercessor between him and men; so he permitted his chosen Daughter, the most Blessed Virgin Mary, to suffer severely, and he received her oblation as an agreeable sacrifice for the advantage and salvation of the whole human race, so that she herself might be a mediatrix between God and men . . . .[17]

In the Vienna *Crucifixion* Triptych, the Virgin offers her sorrow along with her son. Rogier portrayed her tears cascading down her face and mixing with Christ's blood in order to identify her as both the co-redeemer and the Church who presents the oblation of the daily Mass. In this breathtaking painting, he created an overpowering image of the grief that ensured Mary's part in salvation, as well as a literal explanation of the Church's daily sacrifice at the altar.

55. Rogier van der Weyden, *Crucifixion* Diptych, 70 x 72½″ (178 x 184 cm). Philadelphia,
John G. Johnson Collection.

These ideas also dominate Rogier's *Crucifixion* in Philadelphia (Fig.
55). On the left panel of this diptych, the tearful Virgin sinks gracefully
into the arms of Saint John. The theme of her grief, therefore, occupies as
much space as the sacrifice of Christ, which appears at the right. Scholars
have suggested that a missing third panel, on the other side of Christ,
would create a more balanced composition; this monumental conception

56. Rogier van der Weyden, *Descent from the Cross*, 86⅝ x 103⅛" (220 x 262 cm). Madrid, Museo del Prado, on deposit from the Escorial.

seems unchangeable, however, in its equal emphasis on the suffering of both Christ and the Virgin.[18] As in the Vienna *Crucifixion* Triptych, then, Rogier has again dramatized Mary's oblation on Calvary and the essential role of the Church in the Eucharistic rite.

Rogier van der Weyden's Descent from the Cross

Mary's role as co-redeemer is equally prominent in Rogier's unforgettable Prado *Descent from the Cross* (Fig. 56). Many copies of this intensely emotional altarpiece throughout the century prove that it was one of the most imitated compositions of the entire early Netherlandish period. As often remarked, however, it is anything but a historical rendering of the theme. Its dramatic action occurs in the compressed space of a shallow, golden niche rather than on the hill of Calvary, and, as already mentioned, its swooning Virgin falls in an unnatural pose that deliberately echoes the position of the dead Christ.

The Evangelists relate the story of the Descent from the Cross only in connection with the Entombment. According to Matthew (27:57–60), Mark (15:42–47), and Luke (23:50–56), Joseph of Arimathaea took Christ's body and prepared it for burial; John (19:38–42) adds only one assistant, Nicodemus. None of these accounts mention Mary at all, as Parker has recently observed in a provocative study of the problematic sources of the theme.[19] In the *Meditations on the Life of Christ,* however, one sentence describes the Virgin's activity after the removal of the nails from Christ's hands: "Then the Lady reverently receives the hanging right hand and places it against her cheek, gazes upon it and kisses it with heavy tears and sorrowful sighs."[20] This passage may account for Mary's position in other Descents of the period, such as the center panel of Dirc Bouts's triptych in Granada (Fig. 58).[21] It provides no explanation, however, for the awkward posture of Rogier's Virgin.

Panofsky has suggested that Rogier's extraordinary painting was his critique of Campin's *Descent* Triptych, which was probably executed while Rogier was in Campin's workshop.[22] Campin's version is preserved today only in a fragment in Frankfurt, but a faithful fifteenth-century copy of it exists in Liverpool (Fig. 57).[23] In this crowded composition, the figures present Christ's sacrificed body to the viewer as they strain to remove it from the cross. At the left, Mary swoons backwards into Saint John's arms, as the descent down the ladder begins.

In Rogier's panel, on the contrary, the task has already been completed. A quiet, sorrowful ritual replaces the lively action of Campin's scene. Rogier arranged this carefully controlled, rhythmic composition

57. Robert Campin, *Descent from the Cross* Triptych, copy, 23⅝ x 44⅝" (60 x 113.5 cm).
Liverpool, Walker Art Gallery.

around the central Christ, whose reversed position allows the viewer to
concentrate on his side wound.[24] His sacrificed body is, in fact, the abso-
lute center of attention in the picture. Christ neither hangs from the cross
nor rests on the ground, moreover, but remains curiously suspended in
the center of the picture. His raised body clearly corresponds to the Host
that is elevated above the altar during the consecration.[25]

Von Simson's fundamental study of Mary's compassion and co-redemp-
tion in the Prado *Descent* has been mentioned above.[26] Philip has recognized, however, that the Virgin's suffering here conveys another basic
meaning as well: the self-oblation of the Church that occurs during
Mass.[27] As in his *Crucifixion* Triptych, Rogier portrayed Mary here as both
the *Salvatrix Mundi* and the Church who enacts the sacrament of the
Eucharist.

In the Prado *Descent,* however, he also dramatized the reception of
the Host by the congregation. During the late Middle Ages, writers compared the Descent from the Cross with Holy Communion, when the priest
removes the consecrated Host from the altar and presents it to the worshiper. They equated the faithful who receive the "living bread" of the
Eucharist with the recipients of the sacrificed body at the foot of the
Cross. In his famous *Vita Christi,* for instance, Ludolphus declared,

> . . . the faithful communicants [who take] the body of Christ from
> the altar are similar to those who took him down from the cross.
> Indeed, it is even better to take the body of Christ from the altar
> itself than from the altar of the cross. Truly, the latter received him

58. Dirc Bouts, Altarpiece of the Deposition, center panel: *Descent from the Cross,* 75¼ x 61″ (191 x 155 cm). Granada, Capilla Real.

in their arms and hands, but the former take him into their mouths and hearts.[28]

Rogier's painting, therefore, explains the meaning of the rite of Communion as well as the Eucharist. Its grieving figures receive Christ's sacrificed body as the worshipers at the altar below it received the consecrated Host during Mass.

The emphasis on the body of Christ that dominates Rogier's dramatic painting recurs in Descents throughout the period. In the panel by Bouts mentioned above (Fig. 58), for instance, Christ's position seems to echo that of his counterpart in the Prado *Descent.*[29] His torso, which also faces outward to display the side wound, again occupies the central focus midway between the top of the cross and the ground. The grieving figures wait quietly below to receive him, as the congregation awaits the distribution of the Host after the consecration.

The subjects of the reliefs in the archivolt of Bouts's panel clarify its sacramental intent. At the left, the scenes portray the story of Adam and Eve, from the Creation of Adam to the Temptation. They illustrate, therefore, the sin that necessitated Christ's sacrifice. On the right, the Expulsion is followed by Adam and Eve working, the sacrifice of Cain and Abel, and, finally, Abel's murder. As previously mentioned,[30] these last two scenes prefigure Christ's sacrifice.

Although Bouts's scene appears in front of a deep landscape, it is no more historical than Rogier's version at the Prado. It also explains the substance of the Host through the display of Christ's sacrificed body. As in the Prado *Descent,* it involves the worshiper in the intimate contemplation of the meaning of the sacrifice of the Eucharist and its reception by the congregation.

Later Descents with half-length figures focus on Christ's body even more dramatically. In the left panel of Memling's diptych in Granada (Fig. 59),[31] for instance, the half-length format forces the viewer to gaze closely at Christ's bleeding side wound. The right half of this diptych (Fig. 60) concentrates on the grieving Virgin, who is surrounded by the Evangelist

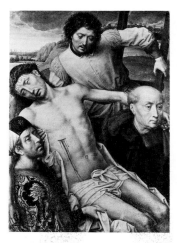

59. Hans Memling, Diptych of the Deposition, left panel, 20¼ x 14¼″ (51.3 x 36.3 cm). Granada, Capilla Real.

60. Hans Memling, Diptych of the Deposition, right panel, 20⅛ x 14⅜″ (51.2 x 36.4 cm). Granada, Capilla Real.

and mourning women. These two panels resemble Rogier's Philadelphia *Crucifixion* (Fig. 55) in their equal emphasis on the suffering of Christ and Mary. As in the Prado *Descent,* however, they also provide a visual explanation of the ceremony of Communion.

Rogier van der Weyden's *Miraflores* Lamentation

The theme of the Lamentation is even less historical than the Passion subjects we have already considered. Although it has no source in the Gospels, it became one of the most popular subjects in early Netherland-ish painting. The most influential version of the Lamentation in this period was the center panel of the Miraflores Altarpiece (Fig. 61),[32] where Rogier created one of his most dramatic explanations of the sacrificial rite. This heart-rending image portrays the tearful Virgin desperately clinging to Christ's rigid body on her lap, while John the Evangelist and Joseph of Arimathaea attempt to comfort her. It differs from earlier interpretations of the theme in the intensity of Mary's suffering.

As noted above, the Evangelists do not include Mary in their accounts of the events leading up to Christ's burial. In the *Meditations on the Life of Christ,* however, a short description of the Lamentation follows the story of the Descent:

> . . . all receive the body of the Lord and place it on the ground. The Lady supports the head and shoulders in her lap, the Magdalen the feet at which she had formerly found so much grace. The others stand about, all making a great bewailing over Him: all most bitterly bewail Him as for a first-born son.[33]

Even this passage, however, does not explain the details of Rogier's intimate scene.

Scholars have frequently studied the popularity of the Lamentation as a devotional theme in late medieval art.[34] They have described the poignant image of the Pietà, in which the Virgin holds Christ's sacrificed body on her lap, as a nonhistorical "Andachtsbild" that encourages the viewer to participate in her suffering.[35] In these discussions, Mary's compassion rarely receives the attention it deserves.[36]

Rogier's dramatic version of the Pietà portrays Mary grasping Christ's stiff, outstretched body with both hands. She presses her face to Christ's cheek so that her tears mingle with his blood, as they do in Rogier's *Crucifixion* Triptych (Fig. 49). This painfully tender figure group became the model for numerous variations by followers of Rogier and by later artists,[37] although its intense emotionality was rarely equaled.

In Rogier's intimate scene, the intertwined figures of the Virgin and

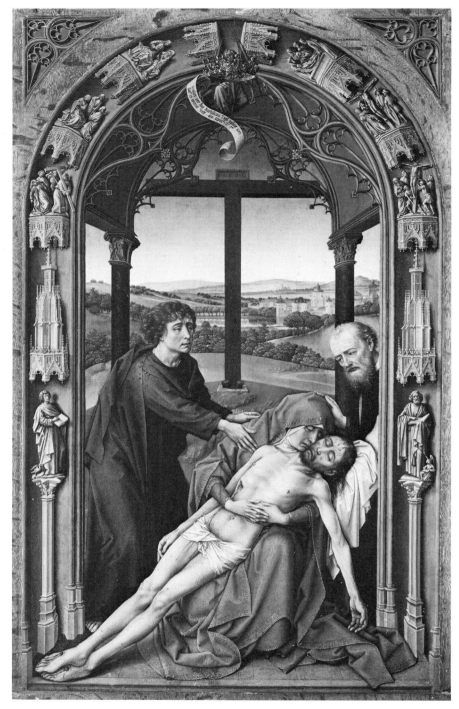

61. Rogier van der Weyden, Miraflores Altarpiece, center panel: *Lamentation,* 28 x 17″ (71 x 43 cm). Berlin, Staatliche Museen Preussischer Kulturbesitz, Gemäldegalerie.

Christ create an unforgettable image of their shared suffering. The central focus on Christ's bleeding body directs the worshiper's eyes to the visual parallel of the consecrated Host. As in Rogier's *Crucifixion* Triptych and Prado *Descent,* Mary simultaneously offers her profound sorrow and her only son. The inseparable figures of the Miraflores *Lamentation* illustrate the physical and emotional suffering that achieves man's salvation and the sacrifice that the Church offers daily in the Eucharistic rite.[38]

Mary is equally important in other Lamentations of the period. In Petrus Christus' version in Brussels (Fig. 62),[39] for instance, she is the focus of the picture. She dominates the space even more dramatically in Christus' similar panel in New York (Fig. 63).[40] Scholars have compared Mary's swooning position in the Brussels version to the deathlike Virgin of Rogier's Prado *Descent,*[41] but they have not explained why she is so prominent in both compositions. In contrast to Rogier's tormented Virgin in the Miraflores *Lamentation,* Christus' Virgin does not touch any part of Christ's body in either painting. She swoons into the arms of her attendants, as Joseph and Nicodemus display Christ's body horizontally across the foreground.

Christus equated the Virgin's emotional torment with Christ's physical suffering, as Rogier did in so many of his Passion scenes. Mary's unusual prominence in these pictures, furthermore, again defines her central role, as the Church, in the daily oblation.

In Christus' paintings, Christ's body rests not on Mary's lap, but on a white shroud that stretches out below her. This unusual arrangement contributes to the sacramental message of the pictures. The body of the sacrificed Christ on a shroud here is as effective a Eucharistic parallel as is the Infant Christ on a swaddling cloth in the Nativities of the period. Just as the altar signifies Christ's manger and tomb, the corporal alludes to his swaddling cloth and shroud.[42]

An even more dramatic interpretation of this analogy occurs in Geertgen's *Lamentation* in Vienna (Fig. 64).[43] Here, Christ's body is also stretched out on a shroud. His back arches stiffly, however, so that only his head and shoulders rest on the Virgin's lap. Mary looks down at him helplessly, without touching him. In this quiet ceremony, her lap serves as the altar on which the sacrifice is laid. The figure placement in this painting enhances its sacramental intent; as Snyder has recognized, the foreground group forms the configuration of a cross, with Christ's body as the shaft and the women as the arms and base.[44]

The emphasis on the shroud in these panels may refer to the cloths that covered the Host in a liturgical ceremony performed at Easter, to be

62. Petrus Christus, *Lamentation,* 38⅝ x 74″ (98 x 188 cm). Brussels, Musées Royaux des Beaux-Arts de Belgique.

63. Petrus Christus, *Lamentation,* 10¼ x 13¾″ (26 x 35 cm). New York, Metropolitan Museum of Art, Gift of Henry G. Marquand, 1890.

64. Geertgen tot Sint Jans, *Lamentation,* 68⅞ x 54¾″ (175 x 139 cm). Vienna, Kunsthistorisches Museum.

65. Robert Campin, *Entombment* Triptych, 23⅝ x 37″ (60 x 93.9 cm). London, Princes Gate Collection (Home House Society), Courtauld Institute Galleries, London University.

discussed presently. As an explanation of the meaning of the corporal, however, the shroud also dramatizes the daily sacrifice.

Robert Campin's Entombment Triptych

As in each of the paintings we have considered in this chapter, Christ's sacrificed body is the focal point of Campin's *Entombment* Triptych in London (Fig. 65).[45] In the emotional central panel of this altarpiece, grieving figures prepare Christ for burial. As Joseph and Nicodemus gently begin to lower him into the sarcophagus, the Magdalen turns her back to the viewer to anoint his feet. Mary bends over him to offer her last kiss, while Saint John reaches out to support her. Two additional holy women busy themselves with the arrangement of Christ's burial cloths, and four sorrowful angels behind and above the main figures hold the instruments of the Passion.

This detailed rendering of the event differs sharply from its description in the Gospels. As noted above,[46] the Evangelists mention the Entombment only briefly in conjunction with the Descent from the Cross. In their accounts, only Joseph of Arimathaea prepares the body, aided, according to John, by Nicodemus. The author of the *Meditations on the Life of Christ,* however, described the event in great detail, including Mary, John, and the Magdalen in his poignant narrative.[47]

The emotionality of Campin's scene could derive just as easily from visual precedents as from the passage in the *Meditations.* Writers have often compared it, for instance, to Simone Martini's small panel of 1342–44 in Berlin (Fig. 66). Campin may even have had first-hand knowledge of this painting, for it was part of a Passion Altar at the Chartreuse de Champmol in Dijon.[48]

Campin's version resembles the Italian panel in its crowding of the figures around the horizontally placed sarcophagus, with some of the mourners in front of the tomb facing away from the viewer. Also similar is the way the Virgin bends to kiss Christ's cheek, although she does not cling to him as she does in Martini's painting. Yet, in spite of the greater emphasis on realistic detail, Campin's painting replaces the landscape with a patternized gold ground that immediately denies the historical tenor of the scene. This gold ground, along with other details that differ from Martini's version, defines the relationship of the painting to the ceremonies at the altar.

In Campin's *Entombment* Triptych, Christ does not rest on the sarcophagus. The grieving figures hold him deliberately above it. As in Mar-

66. Simone Martini, *Entombment,* 9⅛ x 6½″ (23.3 x 16.6 cm). Berlin, Staatliche Museen Preussischer Kulturbesitz, Gemäldegalerie.

tini's painting, this sarcophagus is parallel to the picture plane, as it must have been to the altar that the painting originally adorned. We have already mentioned that writers traditionally associated the altar and Christ's tomb; in the words of Amalarius of Metz (d. 850/51), for instance, "You have here the sepulchre of Christ which you perceive as an altar."[49] The sacrificed Christ above the tomb in Campin's panel parallels the elevation of the Host over the altar at the moment of consecration.[50] In the gold background behind the figures, an unusual raised pattern of grapevines enhances this association, for it refers to the wine of the Eucharist.[51]

As I have suggested elsewhere,[52] the iconographical programme of the *Entombment* Triptych also relates to specific Easter ceremonies performed at side altars that symbolized Christ's tomb. The unusual emphasis on the empty cross behind the supplicant on its left wing recalls the *Adoratio Crucis,* the veneration of the Cross on Good Friday. This ceremony, whose beginnings can be traced to the fourth century,[53] eventually expanded to include the *Depositio* rite. In the *Depositio,* a consecrated Host, often accompanied by a crucifix or effigy of Christ, was "buried" in a receptacle that the texts describe as a *sepulchrum.*[54] Campin's central *Entombment,* with Christ held carefully above the sarcophagus, may reflect the *Depositio.* The *Resurrection* in the right wing, furthermore, seems to echo the subsequent *Elevatio* ceremony of Easter morning, when the Host was miraculously resurrected.[55]

Two cloths, which represented Christ's shroud and headcovering, or sudary, were used to cover the Host in the *Depositio* ceremony; frequently, they were also placed over the cross or effigy. They remained in the *sepulchrum* after the *Elevatio,* to be exhibited later by the three Maries during the ceremony of the visit to the tomb, the *Quem Queritis* play.[56] In Campin's *Entombment,* Joseph and Nicodemus support Christ on an ample shroud; the holy woman behind the Virgin displays a cloth that may refer both to the sudary that covered Christ's head at his burial (John 20:7)[57] and to the sudary used in the *Depositio* rite.

In Rogier's Prado *Descent* (Fig. 56), the body taken down from the cross and received on a shroud by Joseph and Nicodemus may also correspond to the consecrated Host prepared for burial in the *Depositio* rite. The reference to the Easter ceremonies is, however, more pronounced in Campin's triptych, where the Entombment occupies the central position. This emphasis on the Entombment is unusual in paintings of this period, but it occurs frequently in the sculpture groups that Campin's center panel resembles most strongly: the numerous French Entombments that were commissioned for side chapels where their donors were interred. The funerary chapels that these full-scale Entombments decorated were often used for performances of the *Depositio* and *Elevatio* ceremonies.[58] Campin's *Entombment* Triptych may have also adorned an altar in the donor's burial chapel, where it would have dramatized the Easter ceremonies celebrated below it.

Another profoundly moving painting of a similar subject may also relate to the *Depositio* rite. Although it is usually called an Entombment, Rogier van der Weyden's panel at the Uffizi (Fig. 67)[59] bears little resemblance to Campin's scene. It portrays the solemn figures of Mary, John, Joseph, and Nicodemus supporting Christ's erect body in front of a gaping tomb, while the Magdalen kneels with her arms outstretched in an echo of Christ's position. This unusual composition, which Panofsky termed a "Last Farewell Before the Tomb," clearly derives from a painting by Fra Angelico.[60] It differs from its Italian model, however, in the placement of a rectangular slab at Christ's feet. This stone surely represents the cover of the tomb behind the figures, but it probably has a sacramental meaning as well. Graeve has demonstrated that stones of this type often refer to a traditional prototype of the altar, the stone of unction, on which Christ's body was prepared for burial.[61] Thus the stone corresponds to the altar

67. Rogier van der Weyden, *Entombment,* 43¼ x 37¾″ (110 x 96 cm). Florence, Uffizi.

where the priest prepared the consecrated Host for burial during the *Depositio* rite.

As in his other Passion scenes, Rogier has again focused on Christ's sacrificed body. In the Florence *Entombment,* however, his placement of Christ on the stone slab in front of the tomb explains both the meaning of the sacrifice on the altar[62] and the burial of the Host in the *sepulchrum* of the Easter ceremonies.[63]

The Entombment is the final episode of the Passion described by the Evangelists that can be related so explicitly to the daily oblation. Subsequent events of the story occur infrequently in early Netherlandish painting. As we shall see in the following chapter, however, the painters of this period also stressed the theme of Christ's sacrifice in panels that seem far removed from the Passion cycle.

NOTES TO CHAPTER III

1. For the meaning of Mass and the role of the Church in it, see especially Jungmann, I, 175ff. For the dramatic aspects of Mass, see especially Young, I, 81ff., and Hardison, 35ff.

2. For this triptych, which is preserved in the Kunsthistorisches Museum and is usually dated about 1440, see Friedländer, II, #11, and Davies, 240f.

3. Matthew, 27:33–56, Mark 15:22–41, Luke 23:33–49, and John 19:17–37.

4. Ch. LXXVIII; Ragusa and Green, 333ff.

5. As often noted, the composition of this Crucifixion derives ultimately from Duccio's version of the theme in his *Maestà.* For the *Parement de Narbonne,* in the Musée du Louvre in Paris, see Ring, 191, #2; Panofsky, 41ff.; and Meiss, especially 99ff.

6. For this painting, in the Koninklijk Museum in Antwerp, see Panofsky, 36 and fig. 103, and Antwerp, Musée Royal des Beaux-Arts, *Catalogue descriptif, maîtres anciens,* 2nd ed., Antwerp, 1958, 126, #519, where the inscription is printed.

7. Cf. Philip's discussion on 196f.

8. Koninklijk Museum; Friedländer, II, #16. For the suggestion that this cathedral may depict Ste. Gudule in Brussels, and for arguments dating it in the 1450s, see Panofsky, 283f. Cf. also Davies, 196, for statements in support of this date.

9. E.g., in the *Gellone Sacramentary* in Paris (Bibliothèque Nationale, ms. lat.

12048, fol. 143v.); for this miniature, see B. Teyssèdre, *Le Sacramentaire de Gellone et la figure humaine dans les manuscrits francs du VIIIe siècle,* Toulouse, 1959, 108ff. and the color plate following the text. Christ also appears on the cross frequently in Gothic miniatures that illustrate the Canon of the Mass; see, e.g., the English missal of 1311–19 at the Pierpont Morgan Library in New York, M. 107, fol. 142 (Plummer, 25f., #28, pl. 11).

10. For this manuscript (Pierpont Morgan Library, M. 691), see M. Rickert, "The Illuminated Manuscripts of Dirc van Delft's Tafel van den Kersten Ghelove," *Journal of the Walters Art Gallery,* XII, 1949, 79ff., and Panofsky, 98 and n. 98[5].

11. Panofsky, 282, has noted that no earlier depiction of the sacraments had placed them in a church. Cf. the detailed discussion of the Eucharistic symbolism of this altarpiece in Blum, "Symbolic Invention," 111ff. As illustrated in Fig. 53 here, the priest raises not the chalice, as stated in Davies, 195, but the wafer.

12. E.g., in the left wing of Bouts's *Descent* Triptych in the Capilla Real in Granada; for this painting, see Friedländer, III, #2a, and Van Schoute, 36ff., especially pl. LXXV.

13. See, e.g., Panofsky, 267 and 267[3].

14. Von Simson, 13f. For the Virgin's compassion, see also Hirn, 393ff., and Mâle, 122f. In addition to the sources cited by

them, see the homily on Mary's compassion in Amadeus of Lausanne, 138ff., translated into English in Bernard of Clairvaux and Amadeus of Lausanne, *Magnificat,* 99ff.

15. Von Simson, 9ff. For the Escorial version of this composition, now exhibited at the Prado and believed to be the original, see especially Friedländer, II, #3, and Davies, 223ff.

16. E.g., Augustine, *De Civitate Dei* X, 20 (*Corpus Scriptorum Ecclesiasticorum Latinorum,* XL, pt. 1, rpt. of the 1898 ed., Wiesbaden, 1962, 481): "... ipse offerens, ipse et oblatio. Cuius rei sacramentum cottidianum esse voluit Ecclesiae-sacrificium, quae cum ipsius capitis corpus sit, se ipsam per ipsum discit offerre." This passage is cited in Jungmann, I, 190, n. 45, with a discussion of the self-oblation of the Church on 190ff.; see also Philip, 81.

17. *Exercita seu Meditatio Optima Vitae et Passionis Jesu-Christi,* Ch. XVIII (Tauler, VI, 253f):

> Ut enim Pater coelestis unicum Filium suum in ara crucis vivam obtulit hostiam, et quotidie adhuc offert in sacramento pro salute hominum, quo perpetuus esset inter ipsum et homines intercessor; ita electam Filiam suam, Beatissimam Virginem Mariam dure pati permisit, ejusque oblationnem in gratum suscepit sacrificium ad utilitatem et salutem totius humani generis, quo et ipsa perpetua esset mediatrix inter Deum et homines. ...

This passage is quoted in Laurentin, 166f.

18. Panofsky, n. 285², has refuted the theory of a third panel; cf. Blum, "Symbolic Invention," 119. For this painting, in the John G. Johnson Collection, see also Friedländer, II, #15, and Davies, 232ff.

19. Parker, 22f. An excellent discussion of the literary sources of the theme follows in *ibid.,* 23ff.

20. Ch. LXXXI; Ragusa and Green, 342.

21. Capilla Real; Friedländer, II, #2a and 87, n. 25. For the acceptance of the Granada version of this composition as the original and opinions on its dating, see Van Schoute, 36ff.

22. Panofsky, 168f. and 257, where a date of c. 1435 for the Prado *Descent* is implied. For the problem of Rogier's apprenticeship with Campin, see especially *ibid.,* 155f.

23. For the controversy over the identification of the figure as the Good or Bad

Thief in the fragment (Städelsches Kunstinstitut; Friedländer, II, #59), see Panofsky, 168, and Held's review of Panofsky's book, 213f. For the copy in the Walker Art Gallery in Liverpool, in which a blue sky replaces the original gold ground that is visible in the Frankfurt fragment, see Friedländer, II, #59a.

24. I am grateful to Walter Gibson for this observation.

25. Cf. the sacramental interpretations of this scene in Philip, 81, n. 164; Parker, 41f.; and Benjamin, 19.

26. See above, Ch. III, n. 15 and the accompanying text.

27. Philip, 81, n. 164.

28. Part II, Ch. LXV: *De Secundus Vesperis, In Passione Domini* (Ludolphus, IV, 143):

> ... fideles communicantes Corpus Domini de altari, aequiparantur illis qui ipsum deposuerunt de cruce. Perinde enim est, imo plus Christi Corpus sumere de ara altaris, quam de ara crucis. Illi enim acceperunt eum in brachiis et manibus; sed isti sumunt in ore et cordibus.

This passage is quoted in part in Ringbom, 124f., n. 64, and Parker, 98, and referred to in Benjamin, 19. I am grateful to Lotte Brand Philip for first suggesting to me the connection between the Descent from the Cross and the reception of the Host.

29. This was suggested by Friedländer, III, 23. For this painting, see above, Ch. III, n. 21 and the accompanying text.

30. See above, Ch. II, n. 57 and the accompanying text. For the scenes in the archivolt, see also Van Schoute, 38.

31. Friedländer, VIa, #13; for this diptych, in the Capilla Real, see especially Van Schoute, 65ff.

32. For arguments about the authenticity, provenance, and date of the two versions of this work, see, e.g., Panofsky, n. 259³; Van Schoute, 93ff.; Davies, 213ff.; and, most recently, Grosshans, 49ff. The illustration in Fig. 61 comes from the triptych in the Staatliche Museen in Berlin (Friedländer, II, #1a), since the other version, in the Capilla Real in Granada (*ibid.,* II, #1), is mutilated.

33. Ch. LXXXI; Ragusa and Green, 342. The description of Mary's grief also continues in the following chapter.

34. For a summary of the sources of the Lamentation, see E. Lucchesi Palli and L. Hoffscholte, "Beweinung Christi," in *Lexikon,* I, 278ff.

35. See Panofsky, 261f., for the Italian sources of the Pietà. J. H. Emminghaus, "Vesperbild," in *Lexikon,* IV, 450ff., includes a good summary of additional sources and bibliography. For the term "Andachtsbild," see above, Introduction, n. 25 and the accompanying text.

36. The most extensive discussion of Mary's compassion in the Pietà occurs in Dobrzeniecki, 5ff.

37. For the replicas and variants of this Pietà, see especially Panofsky, n. 261[4] and Friedländer, II, #20 and 20a–d.

38. For the thematic relationship between Rogier's Miraflores Altarpiece and Saint John Triptych (Berlin, Staatliche Museen), see Lane, "Rogier's Altarpieces," 669ff.

39. Friedländer, I, pl. 93. For the controversy over the date of this panel, which is in the Musées Royaux des Beaux-Arts de Belgique, see especially Upton, 295.

40. Metropolitan Museum of Art; Friedländer, I, pl. 84.

41. E.g., Upton, 294.

42. Cf. Hirn, 79f.

43. Kunsthistorisches Museum; Friedländer, V, #6A.

44. Snyder, 114.

45. Princes Gate Collection, Courtauld Institute Galleries (formerly Count A. Seilern Collection); Friedländer, II, Add. 147. This discussion of the *Entombment* Triptych is based on Lane, "'Depositio et Elevatio,'" where opinions about its early dating are reviewed in n. 1.

46. See Ch. III, n. 18 and the accompanying text.

47. Ch. LXXXII; Ragusa and Green, 342ff.

48. For this suggestion, see especially G. Troescher, *Burgundische Malerei,* Berlin, 1966, 95, and H. Beenken, *Rogier van der Weyden,* Munich, 1951, 21. The panel is now in the Staatliche Museen.

49. *Eclogae de Officio Missae* (Migne, *P.L.,* CV, 1326B): "Ecce habes hic tumulum Christi quam conspicis aram." For this symbolism, see especially Hirn, 68f. and 492, n. 9; Young, I, 219ff.; Gottlieb, "Living Host," 31f.; McNamee, "Origin of the Vested Angel," 271, n. 23; and above, Ch. II, n. 54 and the accompanying text.

50. Cf. Blum, 9, for a similar interpretation.

51. For the pattern of grapevines, see Van Gelder, 15.

52. Lane, "'Depositio et Elevatio,'" 26ff.

53. For the *Adoratio Crucis,* see especially Young, *Dramatic Associations,* 18ff.; Brooks, 31f.; Young, I, 117ff.; Hardison, 130ff.; and Parker, 99ff.

54. For the problem of the separate burials of the Host and the Cross, see Hardison, 138, and Parker, 84ff. The Host used in this service was consecrated the previous day (Maundy Thursday), since no consecrations are permitted on Good Friday.

55. For the *Depositio* and *Elevatio,* see, e.g., Young, *Dramatic Associations,* especially 8, n. 16, with additional bibliography; Brooks, 168ff.; Young, I, 112f.; Schwarzweber, 61ff.; Hardison, especially 136ff.; Forsyth, *Entombment,* 11; and, most recently, Scheingorn, 50f.

56. For texts of plays of the Visit to the Tomb in which the wrapping for the head of Christ is mentioned, see Young, I, 307ff., and Hardison, 299f.

57. For the wrapping of the head of the deceased at Jewish burials, see Young, I, 134f. As noted by Van Gelder, 13 and n. 41, the traditional identification of this figure as St. Veronica must be incorrect, since she does not belong to the iconography of the Entombment.

58. Documentation for these Entombments appears in Forsyth, *Entombment,* 191ff. See Lane, "'Depositio et Elevatio,'" 24ff., for the similarities between these carved Entombments and Campin's painting.

59. Friedländer, II, #22, and Davies, 212.

60. Alte Pinakothek, Munich. See J. Pope-Hennessy, *Fra Angelico,* London, 1952, 174f., for its probable association with the San Marco Altarpiece, and Panofsky, 273f., text ill. 57, for its relationship to Rogier's painting. Because of this influence, Rogier's panel is usually dated after his trip to Italy in 1450. For a review of opinions concerning this trip, see Lane, "Early Italian Sources," 281 and nn. 2 and 3.

61. M. A. Graeve, "The Stone of Unction in Caravaggio's Painting for the Chiesa Nuova," *Art Bulletin,* XL, 1958, 227ff., with a detailed discussion of the Greek sources of the theme.

62. Cf. *Ibid.,* 232f.

63. It should be noted here that certain altarpieces of the period dramatize still another ceremony of the Easter liturgy, Baptism. For the parallels between this essential sacrament and the Eucharist, and for its inclusion as the major theme of Rogier's Saint John Triptych, see Lane, "Rogier's Altarpieces," passim.

68. Dirc Bouts, Holy Sacrament Altarpiece, center panel: *Institution of the Eucharist,* 70⅞ x 59½″ (180 x 151 cm). Louvain, Collegiate Church of St. Peter.

IV
Priest and Sacrifice

The priest is just as indispensable for the celebration of Mass as the bread and wine. Only he can perform the Eucharistic rite. During the oblation, he recites Christ's words at the Last Supper, and thereby transforms the bread and wine into the body and blood of Christ. At every Mass, therefore, he repeats Christ's action as priest at the Last Supper as well as his sacrifice on the cross.

The Passion scenes that we considered in Chapter III concentrate on Christ's sacrificial body, which usually occupies the central position in the picture. In other early Netherlandish panels, however, Christ frequently acts as the priest who presents the offering as well as the sacrifice itself. The aim of this chapter is to consider some of the most dramatic instances when the painters of the period managed to evoke both ideas simultaneously.

Christ's dual role in paintings of this period is based on a long and well-established tradition. Its ultimate source is the Epistle to the Hebrews, where Christ is extolled as the eternal priest who offers his blood for man's salvation.[1] In the Early Christian period, Augustine emphasized the interdependence of Christ's roles as "priest and sacrifice."[2] The Church officially recognized both functions in 1215, in the opening decree on Transubstantiation of the Fourth Lateran Council.[3]

In support of Christ's priesthood, theologians cited an Old Testament prototype, Melchizedek. Ambrose described Melchizedek as the "author of the sacraments," since, in his meeting with Abraham, he was the first to offer bread and wine.[4] In the visual arts, this offering often prefigures the Eucharist, and Melchizedek sometimes even presents it at an altar.[5] This typology was popularized in the late Middle Ages by the *Biblia Pauperum*

107

and the *Speculum Humanae Salvationis,*[6] in which the Meeting of Abraham and Melchizedek appears beside the Last Supper. In the illuminated *Biblia Pauperum* of the early fourteenth century in Weimar (Fig. 69), for instance, Melchizedek wears priestly vestments and a bishop's miter, and the wafer that he holds above his chalice is actually inscribed with a crucifix.[7] The text beside this miniature explains that the priest, Melchizedek, denotes Christ, and that his offering prefigures the bread and wine of the Eucharist. Similar images appear in the *Speculum Humanae Salvationis,* where the text expands the parallel at length:

Melchizedek was king and priest of the highest God
And he bore a sign of our Lord Jesus Christ:
Indeed, Christ is the king who created all kingdoms
Yet he is also the priest who celebrated the first Mass.
Melchizedek, priest and king, offered bread and wine;
Christ, under the species of bread and wine, instituted
  this sacrament.[8]

69. *Melchizedek as the Prototype of Christ Beside the Last Supper, Biblia Pauperum,* c. 9½ x 13″ (c. 24 x 33 cm). Weimar, Landesbibliothek.

70. *Christ Elevating the Host, Petites Heures du Duc de Berry,* 8½ x 5¾ (21.5 x 14.5 cm). Paris, Bibliothèque Nationale.

71. *Christ Blessing the Wafer and Chalice,* Missal, 11⅞ x 8½″ (30.1 x 21.5 cm). New York, Pierpont Morgan Library.

No single formula for the representation of Christ as priest had developed in northern Europe by the fifteenth century. Some of the most literal portrayals of this idea occur in earlier French miniatures that illustrate the Mass of Corpus Christi. In a series of fourteenth-century scenes of the Elevation of the Host, for instance, a cruciform halo designates the priest as Christ himself: for example, in the previously mentioned miniature of the *Petites Heures* (Fig. 70).[9] Here, curtains separate to reveal the Duke of Berry in prayer near an altar, where the celebrant raises a wafer that is imprinted with an image of the Crucifixion. Other illustrations for this Mass depict a seated Christ holding a large wafer over a chalice, as in a Missal of about 1400 in New York (Fig. 71).[10]

In early Netherlandish painting, artists portrayed this idea in various ways. On the upper story of the interior of Van Eyck's Ghent Altarpiece, for instance, the central figure raises his right hand in blessing (Fig. 72). Although he holds no Host, his elaborate cope, stole, and papal tiara

72. Jan van Eyck, Ghent Altarpiece, detail of Figure 91: *Christ,* 82⅞ x 31½″ (210.5 x 80 cm). Ghent, St. Bavo.

unmistakably identify his priestly role. This majestic figure looms above a sacrificial lamb on an altar in the landscape of the lower story (Fig. 91). He seems to represent Christ as priest, crowning the symbol of his sacrifice on the altar below.[11]

Variations of this image throughout the fifteenth century reveal that artists of the period understood its meaning. Memling adapted the costume of Van Eyck's monumental figure, for instance, in his *Salvator Mundi with Singing Angels* of about 1490 (Fig. 73). The words on the neckband of Christ's alb in Memling's version affirm this identification, for they begin the Lamentations recited by the priest during the Adoration of the Cross on Good Friday.[12]

Other paintings of the period depict Christ as both priest and sacrifice. Although the subjects of these complex works vary greatly, they resemble each other in their portrayal of Christ's dual role.

73. Hans Memling, *Salvator Mundi with Singing Angels,* center panel, 65 x 83½″ (165 x 212 cm). Antwerp, Koninklijk Museum.

Dirc Bouts's Holy Sacrament Altarpiece

In the central panel of the Holy Sacrament Altarpiece by Dirc Bouts in Louvain (Fig. 68),[13] Christ blesses the bread and wine simultaneously, above an empty paschal plate. This solemn scene does not conform to the Biblical accounts of the Last Supper, for it depicts neither Christ's dramatic announcement that one of the apostles would betray him nor his separate blessings of the bread and wine. It portrays a nonhistorical, ritualistic interpretation of the institution of the Eucharist.[14]

Because Christ first consecrated the bread and wine at the Last Supper,[15] this event is ideally suited for the portrayal of his function as priest. Since the priest repeats Christ's words at the Last Supper during the Transubstantiation, the worshiper hears a literal reenactment of the historical event that needs no pictorial explanation. This may be the reason for the infrequency of the Last Supper as a theme in early Netherlandish painting. Bouts's painting is the earliest extant example of it in this period, and most later fifteenth-century versions derive from his composition. His choice of it for the center panel of his triptych results from its commission, as Blum has demonstrated.[16]

The altarpiece was ordered by the Confraternity of the Blessed Sacrament of Louvain, for the larger of its two chapels in the Church of Saint Peter. Although the confraternity had owned this chapel for thirty-one years, its members delayed the commission for its decoration until 1464, the two hundredth anniversary of the institution of the Feast of Corpus Christi. Both the chapel and the confraternity itself were dedicated to this feast. The contract specified a Last Supper with the twelve Apostles in the center panel, as well as four Old Testament prefigurations on the wings.[17]

Bouts's painting relates more closely to traditional Corpus Christi imagery than scholars have recognized. From the establishment of the feast in 1264 on,[18] illustrations of the Corpus Christi Mass emphasized the display of the Host in scenes of the Elevation or the Procession of the Holy Sacrament.[19] In the fourteenth century, however, miniatures with Christ acting as priest also became popular, as illustrated in Figs. 70 and 71. Sacramental interpretations of the Last Supper frequently served as introductions to this Mass as well. This tradition is perhaps best exemplified in a miniature of about 1380–85 from the Milan section of the previously mentioned "Turin-Milan Hours" (Fig. 74).[20] In the main miniature on this page, Christ blesses the wafer and the chalice at the Last Supper. A monstrance displaying the Host in the opening initial and scenes of Confession and Communion in the *bas-de-page* complete the sacramental imagery. This Last Supper is the closest visual parallel to the version by Bouts, who may have derived his composition from a model of this type.

Similar interpretations of the Last Supper exist elsewhere in medieval manuscripts.[21] The frequent use of this theme to illustrate the Corpus Christi Mass,[22] however, suggests that Bouts was familiar with this tradition. His altarpiece continues the sacramental interpretations of the Last Supper that appear in miniatures associated with the very feast to which it was dedicated.[23]

Bouts's painting resembles these earlier miniatures in the depiction of Christ as priest. It differs from them, however, in the symbolic use of the setting. In Bouts's scene, the table acts as the altar over which the first Mass is celebrated.[24] The paschal plate alludes to the paten on which the Host will rest; it is empty because the historical sacrifice has not yet occurred. A liturgical niche with a laver, visible through the doorway, contributes to the identification of the space as a sanctuary.[25]

74. *Last Supper, Heures de Milan,* 11⅛ x 8⅛″ (28.4 x 20.5 cm). Turin, Museo Civico.

75. Joos van Ghent, *Communion of the Apostles,* 130¼ x 131⅞″ (331 x 335 cm). Urbino, Galleria Nazionale delle Marche.

The screened fireplace behind Christ clarifies his sacrificial role in Bouts's painting. In her recent study of fireplace symbolism, O'Meara has described the analogy between such realistic hearths and the Old Testament altar of burnt offerings.[26] As she has noted, Christ's head and shoulders literally replace the fire in Bouts's painting and thereby allude to the Eucharistic sacrifice: ". . . the fireplace becomes the altar that contains the sacrifice of the Cross and the Sacrament of the body of Christ."[27]

Bouts's deliberate placement of Christ precisely at the intersection of the fireplace and the table permits this figure to function on two levels simultaneously. As the sacrifice that replaces the Old Testament immolation, he occupies the center of the fireplace. As the celebrant who performs the sacramental rite in the sanctuary, he officiates at the altar-table.

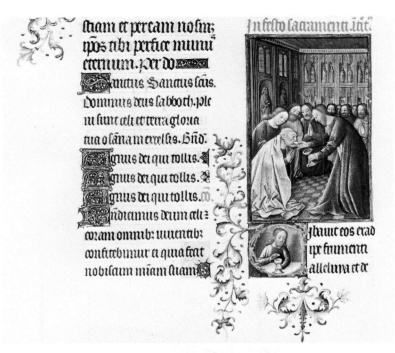

76. *Communion of the Apostles, Très Riches Heures du Duc de Berry.*
Chantilly, Musée Condé.

In its subject and commission, Joos van Ghent's *Communion of the Apostles* in Urbino (Fig. 75)[28] is closely related to Bouts's work. Here, however, Christ stands in front of the table and offers a wafer to the first Apostle. This panel is part of an altarpiece ordered by the Confraternity of Corpus Domini for the high altar of their church of the same name in Urbino. Uccello executed the predella of this work, the *Miracle of the Profaned Host,* in 1467–68, but Joos van Ghent produced its main panel in 1473–1474.[29]

Lavin's perceptive analysis of this altarpiece has designated Christ as priest and sacrifice in it. She has emphasized his ceremonial pose in front of the altar-table, on which the wafers and wine of the Mass rest. Her discussion demonstrates that this work relates to the liturgy of the Feast of Corpus Domini, as the celebration was called in Italy, just as closely as does Bouts's altarpiece.[30]

Whereas the Communion of the Apostles is more frequent in Byzantine art, as Lavin has noted,[31] it does appear occasionally in northern illumination as an illustration for the Mass of Corpus Christi: for example, in a miniature executed by Jean Colombe about 1480 for the previously unfinished *Très Riches Heures du Duc de Berry,* now in Chantilly (Fig. 76).[32]

77. Rogier van der Weyden, Braque Triptych, 13⅜ x 45⅝″ (34 x 116 cm). Paris, Musée du Louvre.

The sacramental intent of this scene is emphasized by its clearly ecclesiastical setting. In the historiated initial below it, moreover, Christ holds a wafer over a chalice as he does in Bouts's central panel.

In Joos van Ghent's altarpiece, Christ offers the bread that signifies his body to his Apostles. This ritualistic scene focuses on the central, dominant figure of the first priest, whose action dramatizes the presentation of the Host to the congregation.

Rogier van der Weyden's Braque Triptych

Christ's sacramental function is less apparent in Rogier's Braque Triptych, at the Louvre (Fig. 77), than in the altarpieces by Dirc Bouts and Joos van Ghent. In this small but grandiose work, Rogier placed his imposing figure of Christ in the central place of honor. The Virgin and John the Evangelist flank him in the center panel, and John the Baptist and Mary Magdalen appear in the wings. These five half-length figures appear before a pastoral landscape and majestically fill almost the total height of their panels. Their solemnity creates the impression of the performance of a sacred ritual.

Although many scholars have extolled this remarkable painting as one of Rogier's most monumental conceptions, few have attempted to define its complex meaning.[33] In most discussions of its theme, writers call it a Deësis, in which the central Christ functions as judge.[34] The figure at Christ's left is not the interceding John the Baptist, as in a usual Deësis group, however, but John the Evangelist, who holds a chalice.[35] Whereas Christ's role as judge may indeed be suggested by the placement of the Baptist next to the Virgin, on Christ's honored right side, judgment is certainly not the major theme of the painting.

Nothing in the simple clothing of Rogier's Christ identifies him as a priest. Later variations of this image, however, always have elaborate liturgical vestments. In Memling's previously mentioned version in Antwerp (Fig. 73), for instance, Christ's priestly garb recalls the costume of Van Eyck's commanding Savior in the Ghent Altarpiece (Fig. 72). His cross-surmounted globe clearly derives, however, from the Braque Triptych. The recurrence of similarly dressed figures in other derivatives of Rogier's painting[36] suggests that the artists of these works recognized Christ's function as priest in the Braque Triptych.

Since Rogier's Christ has several roles in this imposing painting, his garb could not be limited to any one of them. In order to designate Christ's priesthood, therefore, Rogier had to use motifs other than liturgical vestments.

78. Cimabue and others, *Pantocrator*. Pisa Cathedral.

The prominent cross-surmounted globe in the Braque Triptych identifies Christ as the *Salvator Mundi*.[37] Gottlieb has noted that the light in this globe emanates from a "mystical window," the radiant glow of which recalls the metaphor of Christ as the Light of the World.[38]

As I have suggested elsewhere,[39] Rogier's Christ seems to be a variation of those images in which the Redeemer holds a book or a scroll inscribed with the words of John 8:12: "Ego sum lux mundi." This theme occurs often in Italian apse mosaics of the late Romanesque and Gothic periods. Since Rogier executed the Braque Triptych about 1452, shortly after his return from Italy, it may reveal the influence of mosaics of this type.[40] The formal frontality of his Christ figure, in fact, recalls such powerful images as the Pantocrator in the apse mosaic of Pisa Cathedral (Fig. 78).[41] In the Braque Triptych, however, Christ carries a sparkling globe instead of an inscribed book. Apparently in order to convey the idea of Christ as the *Lux Mundi,* Rogier substituted the brilliant light in the globe for the words themselves.

The globe may, however, also have another function in Rogier's painting. In her discussion of its salvational character, Gottlieb has briefly mentioned an earlier tradition in which the globe was conflated with the Eucharistic wafer.[42] This remarkable fusion of ideas seems to have originated in the Carolingian period, as a result of the controversy over the substance of the Eucharist.[43] It is especially prominent in miniatures of Christ in Majesty produced at Tours, such as the one in the *Gospel Book of Lothair* of about 849–51 in Paris (Fig. 79).[44] Here, as in all examples of this type, Christ holds a small disc between his thumb and fourth finger, as the priest holds the wafer in medieval depictions of the Eucharistic rite.[45] In later examples, the disc is sometimes enlarged and transferred to Christ's left hand, resulting in an ambiguous image that may deliberately evoke the associations of both globe and Host.[46] In a tenth-century drawing in Zurich (Fig. 80),[47] for instance, a liturgically vested Christ holds a cross-inscribed disc that conveys both ideas simultaneously.

There is no ambiguity about the clearly modeled globe in the Braque Triptych. Its prominent placement next to the Evangelist's chalice suggests, however, that it may allude to the wafer of the Host. Leprieur and Blum have recognized that Saint John's chalice differs from his usual poisoned cup.[48] Although they have described his image as sacramental, no one has explained his precise function in this painting as Christ's assistant at Mass.

A continuous tradition for the representation of the Evangelist as priest[49] occurs in scenes of his Last Mass, in the so-called "first family" of Apocalypse manuscripts and the blockbooks patterned after them. In the illuminations of the subject, John stands before an altar in liturgical vestments and raises his hands above a chalice that is covered with a corporal, as in an early-fourteenth-century Flemish miniature in Manchester (Fig. 81).[50] Almost identical depictions of the subject appear in the early blockbook versions of the Apocalypse, although in later editions John actually elevates the Host above the chalice.[51]

Rogier's figure of Saint John is not dressed as a priest, because he cannot function as the celebrant in a painting that includes Christ. He seems to act, instead, as the major assistant to the priest, the deacon. Throughout the Middle Ages, it was the deacon who prepared the chalice for the Eucharistic sacrifice and presented it to the celebrant.[52] John holds the foot of the chalice with his left hand in the Braque Triptych, in readiness for presentation to Christ. The unusual gathering of drapery on his left shoulder, moreover, may reflect liturgical practice. Deacons customarily discarded their dalmatics during Lent and Advent for chasubles, which they removed and folded over their left shoulders when they chanted the gospel or administered at the altar.[53]

It cannot be coincidental that both Christ and John raise their right hands in blessing. Their complementary gestures seem to reinforce their

79. *Christ in Majesty, Gospel Book of Lothair,* 12¾ x 9⅞" (32.5 x 25 cm). Paris, Bibliothèque Nationale.

80. *Christ in Majesty,* 9½ x 7" (24 x 18 cm). Zurich, Zentralbibliothek, Ms. C 80.

related functions in the painting. John's attributes designate his role as an assistant in the celebration of Mass and contribute to the interpretation of Christ as priest.

Other features of the triptych define Christ's sacrificial role. Among these, the inscriptions above the heads of each of the figures are the most immediately apparent.

Christ's words, "I am the living bread which came down from heaven" (John 6:51), evoke the idea of the Eucharistic wafer.[54] A desire to convey this meaning, moreover, seems to have led Rogier to choose this specific passage rather than the one from John 8:12 that identifies Christ as the "Light of the World." The use of this passage is extraordinary, if not unique, in an image of the half-length Christ.

The Baptist's inscription, "Behold the lamb of God which taketh away the sin of the world" (John 1:29), identifies Christ as the sacrificial lamb. The priest recites these words, moreover, during the elevation of the Host.[55]

John the Evangelist's statement echoes that of Christ: "And the word was made flesh and dwelt among us" (John 1:14).[56] The beginning of John's first chapter, from which this passage comes, was read frequently as the "Last Gospel" after the Dismissal of the Mass; it occupied this position

81. *John the Evangelist as Priest at His Last Mass, Apocalypse,* 10⅜ x 8″ (26.3 x 20.3 cm). Manchester, John Rylands University Library.

in the ceremony because it summarizes the meaning of the sacrificial rite.[57] Occasionally, the "Last Gospel" was also used as a prayer after Communion.[58]

The Virgin's words of praise from the beginning of the *Magnificat* (Luke 1:46–7) are less directly related to the sacrifice. This passage does occur, however, in the liturgy of Easter week, at the end of the Masses of Maundy Thursday, Good Friday, and Holy Saturday; it was also recited every day at Vespers.[59]

As scholars have frequently noted, the Magdalen's inscription differs from the others, both in its horizontal rather than curving form and in its content, for it is a narrative statement about her rather than a quotation of her own words: "Then took Mary a pound of ointment of spikenard very costly, and anointed the feet of Jesus."[60] Although this passage occurs in John's account of the Supper in the House of Mary and Martha (John 12:3), it describes an action that Christ himself later related to his burial in John 12:7 and Matthew 26:12. Even in this final inscription, therefore, Rogier stressed the theme of Christ's death.

The Magdalen's copious tears (Fig. 82) further clarify Christ's sacrificial function in the triptych. In early Netherlandish painting, she cries only in Passion subjects, as, for instance, in Rogier's *Crucifixion* Triptych in Vienna (Fig. 49).[61] A gospel source for the weeping Magdalen occurs only in John's account, where the angels at the sepulcher and then Christ asks her, "Woman, why weepest thou?" (John 20:13 and 15). Her answer both times expresses concern for the whereabouts of the body of the dead Christ. She also cries often in the chapters on Christ's Passion in the *Meditations on the Life of Christ,* especially at the Crucifixion and preparation of the body for burial.[62] No precedent exists, however, for a crying Magdalen with an image of Christ as judge or Savior of the world.[63]

Frinta is the only scholar to suspect the actual function of the Magdalen in the Braque Triptych. He has recognized that the Magdalen's weeping countenance is out of place with a Deësis, and has proposed that this panel must once have been half of a diptych with a Man of Sorrows. He is so convinced that the Magdalen does not belong with this theme, in fact, that he has insisted that the right panel is not by Rogier at all, but by Robert Campin. His conclusion that the triptych is composed of disparate panels assembled in Rogier's studio is not unlike the traditional arguments concerning the Ghent Altarpiece.[64]

Although Frinta's theory about the execution of the triptych is untenable, his observation that a crying Magdalen would be more suitable with a Man of Sorrows than with a Deësis is indisputable.[65] There is no need to

82. Rogier van der Weyden, Braque Triptych, detail of Figure 77: *Mary Magdalen*.

83. Meliore Toscano, *Christ and Saints*, 33½ x 82⅝" (85 x 210 cm). Florence, Uffizi.

separate the right panel from the rest of the triptych, however, if, as we have seen, the painting does not depict a Deësis at all. Italian sources for the format and figure choice of Rogier's composition, moreover, suggest that he intended to evoke the idea of Christ's sacrifice without depicting him as the Man of Sorrows.

I have proposed elsewhere that the format of the Braque Triptych derives in part from certain Late Gothic Tuscan dossals, whose half-length figures and oblong shape resemble Rogier's painting.[66] The central Christ of each of these dossals is always larger than the figures who flank him, as is also true in the Braque Triptych:[67] for example, in Meliore Toscano's painting of 1271, in Florence (Fig. 83).[68] Rogier's combination of figures, however, differs from these dossals, for John the Evangelist appears at Christ's left only in the example by Meliore.[69] Another Italian source, however, may have influenced Rogier's figure choice.

Half-length images of a central Christ flanked by the Virgin and John the Evangelist abound in fourteenth-century Italian painting and sculpture. The Christ figure in examples of this tradition, however, unlike Rogier's central Christ, is always depicted as the Man of Sorrows.[70] In these works, John the Evangelist invariably stands at Christ's left as a witness of the sacrifice.

Painted versions of this theme usually appear as central predella panels of large altarpieces, with oblong proportions that are similar to those of the Braque Triptych. Several well-preserved examples in and around Florence testify to the existence of this tradition in one of the areas that Rogier probably visited.[71] In some of these predellas, additional saints flank the central three figures, as in the Braque Triptych: for instance, in an altarpiece of 1375 by Pietro Nelli and Tommaso del Mazza in Impruneta (Fig. 84).[72] This example is typical in its depiction of Christ standing in his tomb, with his arms crossed over his body,[73] and in its placement of the Virgin and the Evangelist on either side of him.[74] Similar figure groups occur with less frequency in the main panels of polyptychs and in frescoes.[75]

Carved examples of this tradition occur on Trecento funerary monuments that occupied prominent positions in the churches that Rogier probably visited. In the Tomb of Tedice Aliotti, in Santa Maria Novella in Florence (Fig. 85), for instance, the half-length figures are prominently displayed on the sarcophagus itself.[76] Such reliefs resemble the painted predellas in their carefully separated, half-length figures, their placement of the Evangelist at Christ's left, and their necessarily oblong proportions. All of these characteristics reappear in the Braque Triptych, although

84. Pietro Nelli and Tommaso del Mazza, Predella with Christ as Man of Sorrows, center panel. Impruneta, Chiesa Collegiata.

here, of course, Christ does not reveal his wounds. Yet Rogier may have adapted the format and figure placement of these Italian precedents in order to reinforce the associations with Christ's sacrifice that occur throughout the painting.[77]

Rogier may have been inspired by these Italian sources for another reason as well. Scholars have often suggested that Catherine de Braque commissioned the triptych to commemorate the death of her husband, Jean, in 1452.[78] Recognition of the influence of the Trecento figure groups of the Man of Sorrows on the painting lends support to this hypothesis. Since the carved reliefs of the theme decorate the tombs themselves, their funerary intent is beyond question.[79] The painted predellas of the Man of Sorrows, moreover, were probably also memorials to the deceased donors of the paintings.[80] These sources may have appealed to Rogier precisely because of their associations with death.

Other elements in the painting further substantiate this explanation of the painting's commission. The words in Christ's inscription occur in the liturgy only in the Mass for the Dead.[81] Although the "Last Gospel," from which the Evangelist's inscription comes, could conclude such a Mass, it was also commonly read to the sick before the administration of Extreme Unction.[82] John's liturgical role, furthermore, may have a death-related purpose, for deacons were sometimes permitted to give Communion to the dying.[83]

These references to death raise the possibility that the triptych may have been intended to hang near the tomb of Jean de Braque. Although Catherine still owned the painting at her death in 1499, she may have commissioned it as part of a funerary monument that was never complet-

85. Tomb of Tedice Aliotti. Florence, Sta. Maria Novella.

86. Geertgen tot Sint Jans, *Man of Sorrows*, 9⅝ x 9½" (24.5 x 24 cm). Utrecht, Het Catharijneconvent.

ed.[84] Rogier's apparent inspiration from tomb sculpture corroborates this possibility. The format and symbolism of the painting, then, seem to derive from its original function.

Rogier's exposure to Italian sources did not affect his individual style, but provided him with new ideas to incorporate into a painting of incredible complexity. No work reveals his originality more dramatically than the Braque Triptych, and no painting of the fifteenth century surpasses its powerful, timeless presentation of Christ as priest and sacrifice.

Geertgen tot Sint Jans's Man of Sorrows

At first glance, the small *Man of Sorrows* by Geertgen tot Sint Jans in Utrecht (Fig. 86)[85] seems to concentrate on the sacrificial role of Christ, whose placement close to the picture plane forces the viewer to contemplate his tortured body. In this poignant image of overpowering emotional intensity, blood gushes out of Christ's wounds over his body and down into the tomb in which he stands. With his right hand, Christ indicates the wound in his side, as in innumerable versions of the Man of Sorrows. Yet the tomb and the cross that he clutches with his left arm distinguish the picture from traditional interpretations of this theme, as do the fragmented, grieving figures who surround him.[86]

Snyder has traced the inspiration of this painting to the legend of the Mass of Saint Gregory that originated in the fifteenth century.[87] According to this legend, a vision of Christ as the Man of Sorrows appeared to Gregory while he was celebrating Mass. Fifteenth-century depictions of the legend portray Gregory as the priest before an altar, as in a panel attributed to Robert Campin (Fig. 87).[88] Snyder has explained Geertgen's painting as a transformation of narrative illustrations of this legend into a "re-occurring vision of the Transubstantiation."[89]

Geertgen's painting certainly dramatizes the meaning of the Eucharistic oblation. Whatever its connections to the Mass of Saint Gregory may be, however, it includes no image of Gregory. In it, it is Christ himself who acts as the priest.

Italian images of the Man of Sorrows holding a cross often stress Christ's dual role as priest and sacrifice, as Eisler has noted.[90] In Giovanni Bellini's *Blood of the Redeemer* in London, for instance, Christ's blood pours into a chalice over which he extends his right hand.[91] Eisler has recognized that Bellini's image relates less to the relic of the Holy Blood, as usually suggested, than to the passage in Hebrews that stresses Christ's offering of blood:

> Into the second tabernacle the high priest entered once a year, not without blood, which he offered for his own and the people's sins of ignorance. . . . But when Christ appeared as high priest of the good things to come, he entered once for all through the greater and more perfect tabernacle . . . by virtue of his own blood. . . ." (Hebrews 9:7–8 and 11–13).[92]

In Geertgen's painting, Christ presents his body and blood to the worshiper in a dramatization that must have been intended to portray him as both priest and sacrifice. The picture depicts not only the substance of the Eucharist, but also the celebrant who performs the oblation. Recognition of both of Christ's roles in this painting reinforces Snyder's interpretation of it as ". . . an ingenious pictorial metaphor on the miracle of Transubstantiation that occurs during the Mass."[93]

Images of the Man of Sorrows holding a cross often appear on doors of

87. Robert Campin, *Mass of Saint Gregory,* 33½ x 28¾″ (85 x 73 cm). Brussels, Musées Royaux des Beaux-Arts de Belgique.

Host receptacles in Italian predellas.⁹⁴ The small size of Geertgen's painting (9⅝ × 9½ inches) suggests that it may have served a similar purpose below a large altarpiece. This awesome dramatization of the meaning of the Eucharistic rite could hardly have a more logical function than to cover the consecrated Host itself.

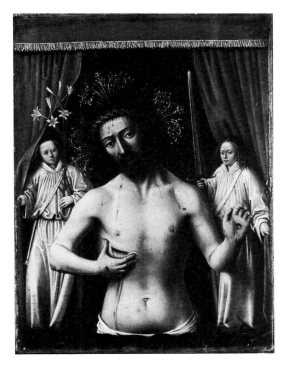

88. Petrus Christus, *Man of Sorrows*, 4½ x 3⅜″ (11.4 x 8.6 cm). Birmingham, England, City Museums and Art Gallery.

Other images of the Man of Sorrows in this period may also express the dual role of Christ. In a tiny panel of the theme by Petrus Christus in Birmingham (Fig. 88), for instance, Christ actively forces the blood out of his side wound and thereby acts, again, as the celebrant who offers the sacrifice.[95] A blue strip at the bottom of this picture may designate the water that flowed from Christ's side and mingled with his blood, as described in John 19:34.[96] Since the water from Christ's wound was traditionally described as the source of Baptismal water,[97] Christus may have intended to evoke the rite of Baptism as well as the Eucharist. A reference to Baptism is perfectly logical in a picture that explains the meaning of the daily sacrifice, since this sacrament is just as necessary for the attainment of salvation as participation in the Eucharistic rite.[98]

As in the other pictures we have considered in this chapter, Christus' panel depicts Christ as both the celebrant and the offering. These incredibly complex paintings dramatize the oblation by illustrating the meaning of the priest's words and actions. They explain to the worshiper that the ceremony he witnesses at Mass signifies Christ's priestly offering of himself as the sacrifice that insures the salvation of mankind.

NOTES TO CHAPTER IV

1. Hebrews 5:6, 5:10, and 7:17 identify Christ as a priest after the order of Melchizedek; Hebrews 9 dwells on the sacrifice of Christ as priest in the tabernacle. For the problematic authorship of Hebrews, see *Oxford Dictionary*, 625ff. The sources for Christ as priest are discussed in H. Skrobucha, "Jesus Hoherpriester," in *Lexikon*, II, 400. See also Purtle, 27ff., for the interrelation of Christ's roles as priest and sacrifice.

2. "Ipse sacerdos, ipse sacrificium" (Augustine, *Sermo 374*, 3; Migne, *P.L.*, XXXIX, 1668); cf. Jungmann, *Mass*, 55.

3. "Una vero est fidelium universalis ecclesia, extra quam nullus omnino salvator. In qua idem ipse sacerdos, et sacrificium Jesus Christus: cuius corpus et sanguis in sacramento altaris sub speciebus panis et vini veraciter continentur . . ." (J.D. Mansi, *Sacrorum Conciliorum Nova, et Amplissima Collectio*, XXII, 1166–1225 [Venice, 1778], facsimile ed., H. Welter, ed., Paris, 1903, 982). Cf. Gottlieb, 74 and n. 37.

4. *De Sacramentis*, Book IV, Ch. 3, 10 and 12 (Migne, *P.L.*, XVI, 438B and D): "Ipse ergo auctor sacramentorum . . . Obtulit ergo Melchisidech panem et vinum." Cf. C. O. Nordström, *Ravennastudien*, Stockholm, 1953, 111.

5. E.g., in the Early Christian mosaics at S. Apollinare in Classe and S. Vitale in Ravenna; for discussions of the symbolism of these mosaics, see *ibid.*, 110ff. (pl. 24c); Von Simson, *Sacred Fortress*, 31; and F. W. Deichmann, "Melchisedek," in *Bild und Verkündigung: Festgabe für Hanna Jursch zum 60. Geburtstag*, Berlin, 1962, 31ff. (figs. 1 and 3). For later examples of Melchisedek at an altar, see G. Seib, "Melchisedech," in *Lexikon*, III, 241ff.

6. For the *Biblia Pauperum*, see especially Cornell.

7. Landesbibliothek, fol. max. 4, fol. 4 v.; H. von der Gabelentz, *Die Biblia Pauperum und Apokalypse der Grossherzogl. Bibliothek zu Weimar*, Strassburg, 1912, pl. 8. Cf. the similar examples in other fourteenth-century *Biblia Pauperum* manuscripts: e.g., Vienna, Nationalbibliothek, 1198, fol. 5 (F. Unterkircher, *Die Wiener Biblia Pauperum*, Cologne, n.d., II, pl. 5r., with the text transcribed in III, 5r., and Cornell, pl. 8) and Salzburg, Benediktinerstiftes St. Peter, ms. a IX 12, fol. 4v. (K. Forstner, *Die Salzburger Armenbibel*, Munich, 1969, fol. 4v., with the text transcribed on 50).

8. Ch. XVI, lines 79–84 (Lutz and Perdrizet, 35):

Melchisedech erat rex et sacerdos
    Dei altissimi
Et gerebat signum Domini nostri
    Jesu Christi:
Christus enim est rex qui omnia regna creavit,
Ipse etiam est sacerdos qui primam
    missam celebravit.
Melchisedech, sacerdos et rex, panem et vinum obtulit;
Christus sub specie panis et vini hoc
    sacramentum instituit.

Cf. the translation of this passage by Blum, 67, where she relates it to Bouts's Holy Sacrament Altarpiece. For the Eucharistic typology of Abraham and Melchizedek in the *Speculum*, see Breitenbach, 170.

9. See above, Ch. I, n. 17 and the accompanying text. Other examples of Christ elevating the Host in this manner include: Lyons, Bibliothèque Municipale, ms. 5122, fol. 185v. (V. Leroquais, *Les Sacramentaires et les missels manuscrits des bibliothèques publiques de France*, Paris, 1924, II, 250f., and G. de Jerphanion, *Le Missel de la Sainte Chapelle à la Bibliothèque de la ville de Lyon*, Lyons, 1944, pl. XXV); Paris, Bibliothèque Nationale, ms. lat. 1052, fol. 157 (V. Leroquais, *Les Breviares manuscrits des bibliothèques publiques de France*, Paris, 1934, III, #511, 49f. and pl. vol., pl. XLIII); and New York, Pierpont Morgan Library, M. 75, fol. 302 (Plummer, #40, 34).

10. Pierpont Morgan Library, M. 331, fol. 156v. For this manuscript, see New York, Pierpont Morgan Library, *Treasures from the Pierpont Morgan Library, Fiftieth Anniversary Exhibition*, New York, 1957, #25, 19.

11. For this interpretation, see, e.g., Philip, 61f.; McNamee, "Origin of the Vested Angel," n. 35; Dhanens, 76; and Purtle, 18.

12. For this altarpiece, originally at Santa Maria la Real in Najera, Spain, and now at the Koninklijk Museum in Antwerp, see Friedländer, VIa, #22. For the identification of the inscription on Christ's neckband, see McNamee, "Good Friday Liturgy," 353ff.

13. For this triptych, still preserved in the Collegiate Church of St. Peter, see Friedländer, III, #18. The most extensive discussion of its commission and sacramental theme occurs in Blum, 59ff. Cf. Panofsky,

318, for a description of its center panel as a "sacred ritual."

14. Cf. Blum, 61ff., and Gilbert, 389. The event is recorded fully in Matthew, 26:17–30, Mark 14:12–26, and Luke 22:7–38.

15. For the Last Supper as the institution of the Eucharist, see especially Jungmann, I, 176ff., and Jungmann, *Mass,* 5ff.

16. See Blum, 62, for the following material regarding the commission.

17. For the scenes on the wings, see especially Blum, 66ff. The contract was first published by E. van Even, "Le Contrat pour l'exécution du triptyque de Thierry Bouts, de la Collégiale Saint-Pierre, à Louvain (1464)," *Bulletins de l'Académie Royal des Sciences, des Lettres et des Beaux-arts de Belgique,* ser. 3, XXXV, 1898, 469ff. For a translation of it, see Blum, 146, n. 43.

18. For the origins of the Feast of Corpus Christi, see especially Hirn, 138ff.; Browe, *Verehrung der Eucharistie,* 70ff.; and Blum, 62f.

19. A brief summary of types of Corpus Christi illustrations in manuscripts occurs in Boom, 326ff.

20. Turin, Museo Civico, *Heures de Milan,* fol. 90; Hulin de Loo, 60, pl. XI. Meiss, fig. 47, attributes this miniature to the Baptist Master. Cf. above, Introduction, n. 14.

21. Dramatic examples without any text occur, e.g., in M. 44 at the Pierpont Morgan Library in New York (mid-twelfth century, fol. 6v.; Loomis, fig. 1) and the *Ingebourg Psalter,* Chantilly, Musée Condé, ms. 1695, fol. 23, early thirteenth century (F. Deuchler, *Der Ingeborgpsalter,* Berlin, 1967, 46ff., fig. 27). In *Speculum Humanae Salvationis* manuscripts of the fourteenth century, sacramental Last Suppers illustrate the passage in ch. XVI that explains the institution of the Eucharist (e.g., Munich, Staatsbibliothek, clm. 146, fol. 18v., reproduced in Lutz and Perdrizet, pl. 31); cf. Breitenbach, 165f.

22. In one unusually explicit example, the Last Supper appears above the elevation of the Host: a fourteenth-century English Carmelite Missal (London, British Library, Add. ms. 29704, fol. 38); see M. Rickert, *The Reconstructed Carmelite Missal,* London, 1952, pl. VI.

23. Blum, 61f., has suggested that Bouts revived a lost early Christian and Byzantine tradition in this painting. The Index of Christian Art at Princeton, however, lists many sacramental Last Suppers of the Middle Ages in addition to those mentioned here. In his review of Blum's book, Parshall,

248, has noted that earlier examples exist in liturgical manuscripts, but he has not connected these scenes with the Corpus Christi Mass.

24. Gilbert, 389, has also recognized that the table functions as an altar.

25. Cf. Blum, 66. For liturgical niches, see above, Ch. II, nn. 8–11 and the accompanying text.

26. O'Meara, 75ff. Cf. above, Introduction, n. 12 and the accompanying text.

27. O'Meara, 84.

28. Galleria Nazionale delle Marche; Friedländer, III, #99.

29. For the commission and sacramental iconography of this altarpiece, see especially Lavin, 1ff.

30. See *ibid.,* 13, where Lavin observes that Christ is designated as the Eternal Priest in the opening antiphon of the first service of the Office of Corpus Domini. Cf. Blum, 144, n. 15, and Gilbert, 389.

31. Lavin, 1.

32. Musée Condé, ms. 65, fol. 189v.; J. Longnon and R. Cazelles, *The Très Riches Heures of Jean, Duke of Berry, Musée Condé, Chantilly,* New York, 1969, #131.

33. For discussions of the triptych's style, see especially Friedländer, II, 19f., #26; Panofsky, 276; and Davies, 21. The most extensive thematic discussion occurs in Blum, 30ff.

34. E.g., Ringbom, 172, and Blum, 32ff. (see also her discussion in "Symbolic Invention," 113). Panofsky, 275, has described it as "not unlike a Deësis," and Frinta, 108, has called it "a Deësis type portrayed in a variation."

35. For the iconography of the Deësis, see especially the discussions by Th. van Bogyay in "Deesis," *Reallexikon zur deutschen Kunstgeschichte,* Stuttgart, 1954, III, 1197ff., and "Deesis," *Lexikon,* I, 494ff. Both Panofsky, 275, and Blum, 33, have recognized that the Evangelist's role is not one of intercession. Blum, 33, has cited precedents for the substitution of the Evangelist in French Gothic carved Deësis groups, but she has admitted that these need not be the sources for Rogier's painting. Cf. Réau, II, pt. 1, 460, and Leprieur, 265f., for other proposals for this substitution.

36. For derivatives by Massys and Joos van Cleve, see Gottlieb, "Mystical Window," 317ff., fig. 7, and Friedländer, VII, #5a and 65 and IX, pt. 1, #34, 34a, and 34b.

37. The most extensive discussion of this theme in Rogier's painting occurs in Gottlieb, "Mystical Window," 315ff.; see

also Ringbom, 172; Blum, 34; and A. Legner, "Christus, Christusbild: Das Christusbild der gotischen Kunst, #6," in *Lexikon*, I, 423f.

38. Gottlieb, "Mystical Window," 315.

39. Lane, "Early Italian Sources," 282.

40. See *ibid*. 281f. and nn. 1–5, for opinions on the triptych's date, on Rogier's trip to Italy in 1450, and on the influence of this trip on his work.

41. Attributed to Cimabue and his school, 1301–2 (Van Marle, I, 453f., fig. 261). Other Italian examples are cited in Capizzi, 329f.). Rogier probably did not know the Italo-Byzantine half-length apse mosaics of Cefalù, Palermo, and Monreale (O. Demus, *The Mosaics of Norman Sicily*, London, 1950, pl. 1–2, 10B, and 61) that derive from half-length Byzantine images of the Pantocrator: e.g., the one at Daphni (O. Demus, *Byzantine Mosaic Decoration*, London, 1947, pl. 7). For examples of the Pantocrator with the citation in question, and the theme as a whole, see Capizzi.

42. Gottlieb, "Mystical Window," 316.

43. This controversy is exemplified in Paschasius Radbertus' treatise of c. 830 on the body and blood of Christ, *De Corpore et Sanguine Domini* (Migne, *P.L.*, CXX, 1267ff.); cf. Schapiro, 343.

44. Bibliothèque Nationale, ms. lat. 266, fol. 2v.; W. Köhler, *Die Karolingischen Miniaturen: I. die Schule von Tours*, Berlin, 1933, 73f. and pl. vol. (1930), pl. 98(b). For additional examples, see Schapiro, 341ff. and figs. 256, 258, and 260. For this tradition, see also Schiller, III, 242 (with additional bibliography cited in n. 23), and Katzenellenbogen, 12 and 108, n. 26.

45. Cf. Schapiro, 343.

46. *Ibid.*, 344f. This double meaning was also proposed by W. W. S. Cook, "The Earliest Painted Panels of Catalonia (II)," *Art Bulletin*, VI, 1923, 58.

47. This drawing (Zentralbibliothek, ms. c. 80, fol. 83) was inserted into a ninth-century manuscript from St. Gall of Alcuin's *Dialectic*; cf. Cook, "Painted Panels," pl. XIX, fig. 33.

48. Leprieur, 266, and Blum, 34. Parshall has objected to the identification of this cup as a chalice in his review of Blum's book, 248. The single example by Bouts (Friedländer III #20) that he has cited as evidence that the Evangelist often holds a cup without the serpent is, however, probably later than Rogier's triptych.

49. For undocumented references to the tradition that John was the first to celebrate Mass in the vestments of a priest, see Blum,

34 and n. 26 on 129; Vloberg, 256; and C. A. Auber, *Histoire et théorie du symbolisme religieux*, Paris, 1884, III, 145. In addition to the examples of the Evangelist dressed as a priest and blessing a chalice discussed below, see the miniature in the *Codex Gisle* of c. 1300 in Osnabrück, Gymnasium Carolinum (Osnabrück, *Codex Gisle*, Berlin, 1926, 44, pl. 35).

50. John Rylands Library, ms. 19, fol. 24v. For this Flemish copy of an English prototype, see M. R. James, *The Apocalypse in Art*, London, 1931, #4, 3. For discussions of the "first family" of thirteenth-century English Apocalypse manuscripts, to which most of the similar renderings of the scene belong, see *ibid.*, 1ff., and L. Delisle and P. Meyer, *L'Apocalypse en français au XIIIe siècle*, Paris, 1910, 11ff. Additional examples occur in Paris, Bibliothèque Nationale, ms. fr. 403, fol. 44v. (James, *Apocalypse*, 2, #1); London, British Library, Add. ms. 35166, fol. 38 (*ibid.*, 4, #9); London, Lambeth Palace, ms. 209, fol. 45 (*ibid.*, 11, #44); and Oxford, Bodleian Library, Auct D. 4. 17, fol. 23v. (*ibid.*, 3, #2, and H. Coxe, *The Apocalypse of S. John the Divine from a Ms. in the Bodleian Library*, London, 1876, xxvi, pl. 23b).

51. Cf. the examples from the second, fourth, and fifth editions in P. Kristeller, *Die Apokalypse*, Berlin, 1916, pl. L, LII, and LIV. See *ibid.*, 54f., #96, for the inscriptions above these scenes, which derive from Voragine's *Golden Legend* (see the Latin text in Jacobus da Voragine, *Legenda Aurea*, ed. Th. Graesse, rpt. of the 1890 ed., Osnabrück, 1965, 63). Most scholars believe the blockbooks were produced in the Netherlands in the middle of the fifteenth century; for a summary of the controversy over their precise dating and provenance, see especially University of Maryland, Department of Art, *The Apocalypse*, text by K. Henkel, Washington, 1973, 76, n. 52. See also the recent reconsideration of the problem by R. A. Koch, "New Criteria for Dating the Netherlandish Biblia Pauperum Blockbook," in *Studies in Late Medieval and Renaissance Painting in Honor of Millard Meiss*, New York, 1978, 285, where the author accepts a date in the second quarter of the fifteenth century for the early editions.

52. Pugin, 116, and *Oxford Dictionary*, 380.

53. Pugin, 117. Complex reasons for this change of vestments are cited in Durandus' *Rationale*, Book II, Ch. ix, 2 and 3 (Barthélemy, I, 190f.).

54. "Ego sum panis vivus q[ui] de c[a]elo

descendi." Cf. Blum, 34, who has recognized that this inscription is Eucharistic.

55. "Ecce agnus dei, qui tollit peccata mun[di]." Cf. *Roman Missal*, 36.

56. "Et verbu[m] caro factu[m] est et habitavit in nobis." Cf. Blum, 34, who has noted the relationship between the two inscriptions.

57. Cf. *Roman Missal,* 39. On the reasons for the use of the Prologue of St. John as the "Last Gospel" of the Mass, see Barthélemy, II, n. 24, 535f., and Jungmann, II, 447ff. Although the usage of the "Last Gospel" varies according to region, and Durandus mentions it only in passing (*Rationale,* Book IV, Ch. xxiv, 5; Barthélemy, II, 130), it does exist in early printed Flemish missals: e.g., in the Liège missals of 1502 and 1513 at the Pierpont Morgan Library in New York (#33052 and 49915). Cf. Jungmann, II, 448, n. 11, for its occurrence elsewhere during the late Middle Ages.

58. *Ibid.,* II, 405 and 405, n. 35. For another use of this passage, see below, Ch. IV, n. 82 and the accompanying text.

59. *Roman Missal,* 461, 501, and 556. Her inscription reads, "Magnificat anima mea d[omi]n[u]m et exultavit sp[iritu]s meus in Deo sal[utari mei]." ("My soul doth magnify the Lord, and my spirit hath rejoiced in God my savior.") For the meaning of the *Magnificat* and its use at Vespers, see, e.g., *Oxford Dictionary,* 858.

60. "Maria ergo accepit libram ung[u]e[n]ti nardi pistici pretioso [sic] et u[n]xit pedes Iesu." Cf. Frinta, 105, and Blum, 34. This passage occurs in the Gospel reading for Monday of Holy Week (see *Roman Missal,* 414). It should be noted that the Gospels do not definitely identify the Mary of this passage with the Magdalen, although until recently this identification was generally accepted (see, e.g., *Oxford Dictionary,* 884).

61. For this triptych, see above, Ch. III, pp. 80–86.

62. E.g., in Ch. LXXVIII and LXXXII; Ragusa and Green, 335 and 343.

63. For the iconographic type of the penitent Magdalen, which became popular only in the later fifteenth century, see Réau, III, pt. 2, 850f.; J. Braun, *Tracht und Attribute der Heiligen in der Deutschen Kunst,* Stuttgart, 1943, 497; and M. Anstett-Janssen, "Maria Magdalena," in *Lexikon,* VII, 518f.

64. Frinta, 108. This theory was convincingly refuted by M. Sonkes, "Le Dessin sous-jacent chez Roger van der Weyden et le problème de la personnalité du Maître de Flémalle," *Bulletin de l'Institut Royal du Patrimoine Artistique,* XIII, 1971–72, 161ff. For a review of the arguments about the separation of hands in the Ghent Altarpiece, see, e.g., Panofsky, 217ff.

65. It must be noted, however, that no diptychs of a half-length Magdalen and Man of Sorrows seem to exist.

66. Lane, "Early Italian Sources," passim.

67. Only Blum, 32, and again in "Symbolic Invention," 113, has noted that Christ's head is higher than the others.

68. Uffizi. For this example, see Van Marle, I, 296, fig. 149a; E. B. Garrison, *Italian Romanesque Panel Painting,* Florence, 1949, 160, #417; and Hagar, 110, fig. 157.

69. Two of the dossals of this group, in fact, depict a Deësis proper; see Lane, "Early Italian Sources," figs. 5 and 7.

70. The frequency of this tradition in Italy has been noted by Mâle, 102, who has interpreted it as signifying Christ's Eternal Passion. Among the rare northern examples before 1450 is the Parisian tapestry of about 1410 at the Musée des Beaux-Arts in Chartres; for this tapestry, see Vienna, Kunsthistorisches Museum, *Europäisches Kunst um 1400,* Vienna, 1962, 475, #531, pl. 41. In this example, John the Baptist appears beside the Virgin, pointing to Christ as he does in the Braque Triptych.

71. This tradition occurs elsewhere in Italy as well. For examples in Sienese painting, see Stubblebine, 8f. See also *ibid.,* 5ff., where the author challenges traditional opinions about the Byzantine origins of the theme of the Man of Sorrows.

72. Collegiate Church; Van Marle, III, 646ff., fig. 366. See also H. D. Gronau, "The San Pier Maggior Altarpiece: a Reconstruction," *Burlington Magazine,* LXXXVI, 1945, pl. III(a) and 143.

73. See also the examples by Taddeo Gaddi and his school, in the Uffizi (Van Marle, III, 343f.), and Nardo di Cione, in the Narodni Galerie in Prague (H. D. Gronau, *Andrea Orcagna and Nardo di Cione,* Berlin, 1937, fig. 51).

74. The infrequent exceptions to this formula include Simone Martini's altarpiece of 1320 in the Museo Civico in Pisa (G. Paccagnini, *Simone Martini,* Milan, 1955, fig. 16), where the Baptist appears on Christ's left.

75. For examples in the main panels of polyptychs, see Stubblebine, 9ff., where a reconstruction of an altarpiece of this theme by Segna di Buonaventura is proposed. A

fresco of the subject by Giovanni Toscani exists at Sta. Trinita in Florence (R. Fremantle, *Florentine Gothic Painters from Giotto to Masaccio,* London, 1975, fig. 1041).

76. First half of the fourteenth century, variously attributed to Tino di Camaino or Maso di Banco (A. Venturi, *Storia dell'arte italiana, IV: la scultura del trecento,* Milan, 1906, 266ff., fig. 194; W. R. Valentiner, *Tino di Camaino,* Paris, 1935, 67, fig. 17; and W. R. Valentiner, "Orcagna and the Black Death of 1348," *Art Quarterly,* XII, 1949, 53f.). At Sta. Croce in Florence, Rogier could have seen the Pazzi Tomb, attributed to Alberto di Arnoldo (Venturi, *Storia,* IV, 300, fig. 216, and Valentiner, *Tino di Camaino,* 65, fig. 16, where it is dated about 1350), and the Baroncelli Tomb by Giovanni di Balduccio (H. Bodmer, "Una scuola di scultura fiorentina nel trecento: i monumenti dei Baroncelli e dei Bardi, I," *Dedalo,* X, 1929–30, 619ff., figs. on 617 and 624–27, where it is dated between 1332 and 1338, and Venturi, *Storia,* IV, 544f., fig. 433). Examples of this tradition occur elsewhere in Italy as well.

77. Rogier's painting is closer to these tomb reliefs than to carved images of the theme on sacrament tabernacles of the fifteenth century (e.g., Desiderio da Settignano's tabernacle of 1461 in S. Lorenzo in Florence; Caspary, fig. on 196). In such examples, which date later than the Braque Triptych, the Virgin and St. John usually support Christ's body, and the figures are, therefore, not as carefully separated from each other as in the Trecento reliefs or Rogier's painting. The location of these later reliefs on receptacles of the reserved Host, however, substantiates the sacramental nature of the theme.

78. E.g., Leprieur, 276, and Blum 29f. For the iconography of the exterior wings, closely related to death, see Leprieur, 261ff., and Blum, 30f.

79. Blum, 30, has proposed an influence of funerary sculpture on the exterior wings; recognition of these Italian sources reinforces her theory.

80. Cf. Walters Art Gallery, *The International Style,* Baltimore, 1962, 11.

81. *Roman Missal,* [231].

82. Jungmann, II, 447.

83. Cf. Freestone, 224f.

84. Leprieur, 275, and Blum, 29 and 31, have stated that it was used in a private domestic chapel and was never intended to adorn the tomb of the deceased. No documents exist, however, that describe its original purpose.

85. Catharijneconvent (formerly Aartsbisschoppelijk Museum); Friedländer, V, #7.

86. For the theme of the Man of Sorrows, see especially Panofsky, "Imago Pietatis," passim. Cf. the more recent considerations of its problematic aspects in Stubblebine, 5ff., and Eisler, lllff. and n. 24, where earlier bibliography is cited.

87. Snyder, 124. For the fifteenth-century records of the Mass of St. Gregory, see especially C. Bertelli, "The 'Image of Pity' in Santa Croce in Gerusalemme," in *Essays in the History of Art Presented to Rudolf Wittkower,* London, 1967, 46ff.

88. Brussels, Musées Royaux des Beaux-Arts de Belgique; Friedländer, II, Add. 150, and Davies, 246f. See also Fig. 44 here, and above, ch. II, n. 23.

89. Snyder, 124.

90. Eisler, passim.

91. For Eisler's comments on this painting, which is at the National Gallery, see *ibid.,* 235, fig. 28.

92. *Ibid.,* 235. For the association of Bellini's painting with the relic of the Holy Blood, see the sources cited in *ibid.,* nn. 98 and 100.

93. Snyder, 123. Cf. Caspary, 105, for the characterization of images of the Man of Sorrows as both priest and sacrifice. Debra Berendt first proposed this interpretation of Geertgen's painting in a seminar at Queens College.

94. See the examples listed in U. Middeldorf, "Un rame inciso del Quattrocento," in *Scritti di storia dell'arte in onore di Mario Salmi,* II, Rome, 1962, 277–79. Eisler, 236, and G. Robertson, *Giovanni Bellini,* Oxford, 1968, 34, both have suggested that Bellini's "Blood of the Redeemer" had this function.

95. City Museums and Art Gallery (Friedländer, I, pl. 108B). Cf. the identification of this Christ figure as Redeemer and judge in J. Rowlands, "A Man of Sorrows by Petrus Christus," *Burlington Magazine,* CIV, 1962, 419.

96. For this blue strip, see Upton, 137f.

97. For the relationship between Baptismal water and the blood from Christ's side wound, see Lane, "Rogier's Altarpieces," 669f.

98. See *ibid.,* 666ff., for the role of Baptism in salvation and for the parallels between Baptism and the Eucharist in two other works of the period, Rogier's Miraflores Altarpiece and Saint John Triptych.

Conclusion

The Promise of the Mass
in Van Eyck's Ghent Altarpiece
and Van der Weyden's
Beaune *Last Judgment*

The fifteenth-century worshiper believed that participation in the earthly Mass insured his reception into heaven. When he saw himself portrayed in a painting that illustrated his involvement in the Mass on earth, he also saw a visual explanation of the way to salvation.

The two most ambitious projects of the period, Van Eyck's Ghent Altarpiece (Figs. 89 and 91) and Rogier van der Weyden's *Last Judgment* Altarpiece in Beaune (Figs. 90 and 92), are unsurpassed in their dramatizations of the relationship between the earthly ceremony and its ultimate promise. Scholars have carefully studied the iconography of each of these incredibly complex works, but they have barely suggested how they relate to each other.[1] The aim of this conclusion is to explore how their thematic parallels summarize the relationship between the altar and the altarpiece that we have traced throughout the period.

Scholars have occasionally noted the similarity of the exteriors of these two monumental works (Figs. 89 and 90).[2] In each altarpiece, the Annunciation appears in the upper panels, above kneeling supplicants who worship statues of saints. Blum has suggested that this resemblance may have resulted from Rogier's fulfillment of the donor's wishes.[3] The Beaune *Last Judgment,* Rogier's largest folding altarpiece,[4] may have been intended to rival the glory of Jan's grandiose work.

Both Jan and Rogier deliberately separated their worshipers from the space of the holy figures. In Jan's Annunciation, the figures occupy an interior setting that is spread across four panels. This deep space contrasts with the shallow niches on the lower story, where Jodocus Vijd and his wife kneel in adoration before Saints John the Baptist and John the Evangelist. In Rogier's altarpiece, small grisaille figures of Mary and the angel

89. Jan van Eyck, Ghent Altarpiece, exterior, 137¾ x 87″ (349.9 x 221 cm). Ghent, St. Bavo.

90. Rogier van der Weyden, *Last Judgment* Altarpiece, exterior, 86⅝ x 107½″ (220 x 273 cm). Beaune, Hôtel-Dieu.

appear in niches on the upper level, above Saints Sebastian and Anthony. Nicolas Rolin and his wife flank the saints in shallow interiors, where they each worship at a prie-dieu. Rogier's use of grisaille for all of the holy figures creates a more deliberate distinction between their space and the space of the human supplicants.

The Annunciation appears on the exterior of these works, as it does so often in this period, because of its inherent connection with the Transubstantiation. In both altarpieces, the worshipers kneel below the visual explanation of the miraculous transformation that occurs in every Mass, when the Holy Spirit changes the Eucharistic wafer into the body of Christ. The donors appear in the view that depicts the Annunciation, because they participate in the earthly ceremony that it explains. They occupy individual spaces that make it possible for them to see the holy figures without entering their sacred realm.

Whereas the exteriors of these two altarpieces explain the participation of the donors at Mass, the interiors (Figs. 91 and 92) portray the

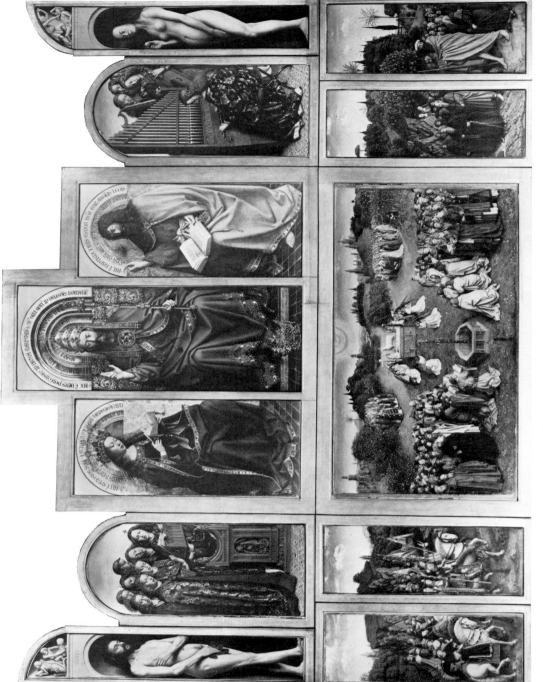

91. Jan van Eyck, Ghent Altarpiece, interior, 137¾ x 181" (349.9 x 459.7 cm). Ghent, St. Bavo.

92. Rogier van der Weyden, *Last Judgment* Altarpiece, interior, 86⅝ x 215¾″ (220 x 548 cm). Beaune, Hôtel-Dieu.

ultimate consequence of participation in the daily sacrifice. In each case, an otherworldly image of breathtaking radiance unfolds when the wings are opened. As in many folding altarpieces of this period, the glowing colors of the glorious visions on the interiors contrast sharply with the relatively subdued tones on their outer views.[5] Smith has persuasively argued that the cool coloration of such exteriors may have resulted from the need to cover the brilliant images of the main views during Lent.[6] By means of this contrast, however, both Jan and Rogier have also suggested the progression from the daily ceremony of Mass on the exterior to its celestial promise in the opened view.

Rogier may have echoed the Ghent Altarpiece on the interior of his polyptych as well as on its exterior. Whereas his interior clearly portrays the Last Judgment, however, the opened view of the Ghent Altarpiece contains many complicated levels of meaning. As mentioned in Chapter IV, Jan's imposing central figure of Christ wears liturgical vestments that identify him as a priest, and the lamb on the altar below him refers to his sacrificial role. He does not display his wounds as Rogier's central Christ does, but his similar placement between the Virgin and John the Baptist suggests that he also functions as judge. Scholars have proposed, in fact, that the Last Judgment is one of the major themes of the Ghent interior.[7]

The appearance of this subject in the Beaune altarpiece supports this interpretation. Rogier may have deliberately condensed the meaning of the Ghent interior in order to present Rolin with a concise image of Christ's second coming. It is probable, moreover, that Rogier also intended to refer to Christ's role as priest, since the archangel below him wears the vestments of a deacon at High Mass.[8] The display of his wounds, moreover, immediately evokes his sacrifice.

The altarpieces are also similar in their commissions. We know that both Vijd and Rolin established Masses for the salvation of their souls in the chapels for which they had ordered their paintings.[9] Vijd and his wife may have planned to be buried beneath Van Eyck's work in their chapel in Saint Bavo's Cathedral.[10] Although Nicolas Rolin eventually selected Autun as his burial place, he originally intended the chapel in the Hôtel-Dieu at Beaune to house both his own grave and that of his wife,[11] below the painting that Rogier executed for him. The *Last Judgment* Altarpiece was, however, also a memorial for the deceased patients in the hospital cemetery.[12] It decorated the altar at the end of the long "Salle des Pauvres," where it presented the sick with an optimistic vision of their eventual reception into Paradise.[13]

In both altarpieces, the visual explanation of the parallel between the Incarnation and the Transubstantiation on the exterior leads directly to the fulfillment of the promise of the Mass, the redemption of mankind, which appears when the wings are opened.[14] The scenes on the interiors represent, in effect, a vision of the salvation that the donors believed they would obtain through participation in the daily sacrifice.[15] Although Vijd and Rolin probably viewed their donation of these altarpieces as extra insurance for their reception into Paradise, they certainly understood that this reception would have been impossible without their involvement in the earthly ceremony of Mass.

The Ghent Altarpiece and the Beaune *Last Judgment* present the viewer with eloquent dramatizations of the celestial rewards he will receive as a result of his earthly piety. Like each of the works we have considered here, they illustrate the meaning of the Eucharistic oblation that occurs during the ceremony of Mass. In their combined views, however, they also portray the ultimate goal of this daily ritual. Whereas the exteriors explain the donors' participation in Mass, the interiors promise the eventual salvation that will result from this participation.

Early Netherlandish altarpieces all convey this promise of salvation. No understanding of any of these radiant paintings is possible without the realization that they had to illustrate the meaning of the sacrifice of the Mass and its related rituals. They were liturgical objects that enhanced the experience of the worshiper with visual explanations of the ceremonies he witnessed. Their extraordinary impact results, in part, from their powerful dramatizations of the rites performed at the altars they adorned.

NOTES TO CONCLUSION

1. The enormous body of literature on these problematic paintings cannot be reviewed here. For the Ghent Altarpiece, finished in 1432, see especially the recent studies by Dhanens and Philip. For the *Last Judgment* Altarpiece, finished by 1452 for the Hôtel-Dieu (where it still remains), see Blum, 37ff.; Davies, 197ff.; and especially Veronee-Verhaegen, passim, where sources that compare the two works briefly are cited on 30.

2. E.g., Panofsky, 268; Blum, 39; and Veronee-Verhaegen, 45.

3. Blum, 39.

4. The *Last Judgment* Altarpiece is 18 feet wide in the opened position; see Veronee-Verhaegen, 3, for measurements of the individual sections. It is, therefore, almost 3 feet wider than the opened Ghent Altarpiece; for exact measurements of the panels in Ghent, see Dhanens, 147.

5. Cf. Blum, 39.

6. Smith, 43ff.

7. See, e.g., Philip, 98ff.

8. Cf. Veronee-Verhaegen, 51.

9. For the deed of 1435 that describes Vijd's wishes, see Dhanens, 24. For Rolin's statutes regarding daily masses, see Blum, 45f. It should be noted that Rolin donated the entire hospital as well as the altarpiece.

10. For this possibility, see especially Philip, 209f. For Vijd's unknown burial place and his wife's grave at the Augustinian monastery in Ghent, see Dhanens, 42.

11. Cf. Blum, 45, and Veronee-Verhaegen, 51.

12. *Ibid.,* 51.

13. See *ibid.,* pl. 1, for a view of the altarpiece when it was temporarily reinstalled on the altar in this room.

14. For the relationship between the exterior and the interior of the Ghent Altarpiece, see especially Philip, 91, and Purtle, 16ff. For the Last Judgment as a drama of Redemption in Rogier's altarpiece, see especially Veronee-Verhaegen, 50.

15. Cf. Blum, 48, where the *Last Judgment* Altarpiece is described as "one of the most overt wish fulfillments of the fifteenth century." Veronee-Verhaegen, 51, discusses the liturgical significance of the Last Judgment as the source of eternal life.

Glossary of Ecclesiastical Terms

Cross references are indicated by words in capitals.

Adoratio Crucis A medieval LITURGICAL ceremony held on GOOD FRIDAY, during which a cross was venerated in commemoration of Christ's Crucifixion.

Advent The period of the church year immediately preceding Christmas, beginning four Sundays before it.

Alb A floor-length white linen garment with long sleeves, worn by all members of the clergy participating in MASS.

Altar The table at which the ceremony of MASS is celebrated.

Altarpiece A painted or carved work of art placed above an ALTAR.

Amice A square or oblong linen cloth, worn around the neck by the PRIEST and subministers at MASS.

Annunciation The announcement of the INCARNATION of Christ by the Archangel Gabriel to the Virgin Mary (Luke 1:26–38). The Feast of the Annunciation, celebrated on March 25, commemorates this event.

Apse A projection at the eastern end of a BASILICA, usually semicircular in shape, where the ALTAR is traditionally placed.

Aumbry A recess in the wall of a medieval church, used to display the receptacle containing the CONSECRATED HOST.

Baldachin, or Baldacchino A free-standing canopy that covers the ALTAR in a Catholic church, usually supported on four pillars. See CIBORIUM.

Baptism The SACRAMENT that admits the worshiper to the Catholic Church and insures his SALVATION. The belief that one buries his sins in the water and emerges in a purified state during this rite persisted even when total immersion was no longer practiced. Because of its symbolic repetition of Christ's death and RESURRECTION, Baptism was traditionally performed on HOLY SATURDAY. The Baptismal water is believed to derive from the water that issued from the side wound of Christ.

Basilica A church of longitudinal plan, usually with a long central NAVE, side aisles, and an APSE at the eastern end.

Bishop The highest rank of minister in the Catholic Church, who governs a particular DIOCESE. The bishop is distinguished from the PRIEST by his

145

power to perform the SACRAMENTS of HOLY ORDERS and CONFIRMATION.

Candlemas The feast, celebrated on February 2, that commemorates the Presentation of Christ in the Temple and the Purification of the Virgin.

Canon (of the Mass) The climax of the MASS, including the prayers leading up to and immediately following the CONSECRATION.

Canticle A song or prayer derived from the Bible, used in LITURGICAL worship.

Cathedral The church that contains the BISHOP's throne (the "cathedra") and hence the most important and usually most elaborate church of the DIOCESE.

Celebrant The PRIEST or BISHOP who officiates at MASS.

Chalice In the Catholic Church, the container of the CONSECRATED wine of the EUCHARIST.

Chasuble An oval, sleeveless garment with a hole in the center for the head, worn by the PRIEST over his other vestments at MASS.

Ciborium The canopy, usually supported on four pillars, that covers the ALTAR in a Catholic church. Also known as a BALDACHIN. The word is sometimes also used to describe a container of the CONSECRATED HOST.

Communion The offering of the CONSECRATED WAFERS of the EUCHARIST by the PRIEST to the congregation.

Communicant A worshiper who receives the CONSECRATED WAFER of the EUCHARIST from the PRIEST during COMMUNION.

Confirmation The SACRAMENT during which the BISHOP confers the grace of the Holy Spirit upon those who have been baptized.

Consecration The ceremony in which the bread and wine of the EUCHARIST are transformed into the Body and Blood of Christ. To CONSECRATE means

to perform this act. The CONSECRATED HOST is the WAFER that is transformed during this ceremony.

Cope A cloak-shaped garment, fastened in the front and worn over the other LITURGICAL vestments by the PRIEST (when the CHASUBLE is not used) and by the subministers at MASS. It can also be worn during ceremonial processions.

Corporal A white linen cloth placed on the ALTAR, on which the bread and wine rest during the EUCHARISTIC rite.

Corpus Christi, Feast of (called Corpus Domini in Italy) The feast that commemorates the institution of the EUCHARIST. Established in 1264 by Pope Urban IV, it is celebrated on the Thursday after Trinity Sunday.

Crucifix A carved or painted image of Christ on the cross, distinguished from the Crucifixion by the absence of any historical details or setting.

Dalmatic A tunic with wide sleeves and a slit up the sides, worn by the DEACON at MASS.

Deacon The rank of clergy below the PRIEST. Among his other duties is his function as the PRIEST's assistant at MASS.

Deësis A representation of the enthroned Christ, flanked by the two major intercessors for mankind: the Virgin Mary and John the Baptist.

Depositio A medieval LITURGICAL ceremony performed on GOOD FRIDAY, during which the CONSECRATED HOST was "buried" in a receptacle, or *SEPULCHRUM*, that symbolized Christ's tomb.

Diocese The territory governed by the BISHOP, including all of the churches under his supervision.

Diptych As used in this study, a two-paneled ALTARPIECE whose panels are usually hinged together.

Dossal A low, wide painting, often composed of several panels joined together, that is placed on top of the back section of the ALTAR.

Easter The celebration of Christ's RESURRECTION, the oldest feast of the Catholic Church.

Elevatio A medieval LITURGICAL ceremony performed on EASTER morning, during which the CONSECRATED HOST that had been "buried" in the *DEPOSITIO* ceremony of GOOD FRIDAY was miraculously resurrected.

Elevation The raising of the HOST and CHALICE by the CELEBRANT as he CONSECRATES them during the EUCHARISTIC rite.

Epiphany The feast, celebrated on January 6, that commemorates the Adoration of the Magi. Since the three Kings represent all nations and races, their adoration of the Child signifies his manifestation to the Gentiles.

Eucharist The SACRAMENT instituted by Christ at the Last Supper, during which he designated the bread and wine as his Body and Blood. The term "Eucharistic" refers to this SACRAMENT. The "Eucharistic rite" is the ceremony of CONSECRATION itself.

Extreme Unction The SACRAMENT of anointing the sick. In the Middle Ages, it was usually reserved for the dying.

Gloria in Excelsis The title of a hymn sung during the CANON of the MASS, deriving its title from its beginning words in Latin.

Good Friday The Friday before EASTER, on which Christ's Crucifixion is commemorated.

Gospel The history of Christ's life and teaching as recorded in the first four books of the New Testament, traditionally attributed to the Evangelists Matthew, Mark, Luke, and John.

Holy Orders The higher ranks of the Catholic ministry, and the SACRAMENT during which the BISHOP confers these ranks.

Holy Saturday The day before EASTER Sunday, commemorating Christ's Entombment. This day was the traditional time for the administration of BAPTISM, since this SACRAMENT symbolically parallels the death and RESURRECTION of Christ.

Host The CONSECRATED WAFER of the EUCHARIST, understood in Catholic theology as the sacrificed body of Christ. The word derives from the Latin *hostia,* which means "sacrificial victim."

Incarnation The doctrine of the birth of Christ in human form as the son of the Virgin Mary. The term "Christ incarnate" refers to Christ's presence on earth in human form.

Intercession The mediation of a saint on behalf of a worshiper. When a saint intercedes, he or she offers a prayer for the supplicant, and this prayer is intercessory in nature. An intercessor is someone who pleads on behalf of the worshiper.

"Last Gospel" The GOSPEL passage read by the DEACON at the end of the MASS.

Laver A container of water used for the washing of the PRIEST's hands before and after MASS.

Liturgy A collection of prayers and ceremonies used for public worship. In the Roman Catholic Church, the word refers especially to the ceremonies of MASS. The term "liturgical" signifies anything related to the performance of these ceremonies.

Magnificat The song of praise recited by the Virgin Mary at the Visitation, in response to Elizabeth's recognition of her as the mother of God. The name derives from the first word of the song in the Latin version of the Gospel of Luke (Luke 1:46–55). As a CANTICLE, it is sung at VESPERS.

Mandorla The Italian word for "almond," used to describe an oval radiance of light surrounding a holy figure and designating divinity.

Manna The bread that was miraculously delivered to the Israelites in the wilderness during their journey from Egypt to the Holy Land (Exodus 16). Throughout the Middle Ages, it was considered a prototype of the bread of the EUCHARIST.

Mass The celebration of the EUCHARIST, during which the sacrifice of Christ on the cross is repeated. Derived from the Latin *missa*.

Maundy Thursday The Thursday before EASTER Sunday. During the MASS on this day, the WAFERS for the Mass on GOOD FRIDAY are CONSECRATED, since no consecrations are permitted on GOOD FRIDAY itself.

Mensa The Latin word for the table of the ALTAR.

Missa Aurea The Golden Mass, a medieval LITURGICAL drama commemorating the ANNUNCIATION and performed on Ember Wednesday of ADVENT (the Wednesday after December 13), immediately preceding the Christmas season.

Missal A LITURGICAL book containing all the prayers and ceremonies of MASS, with directions for their various readings and performances throughout the year.

Miter (or mitre) The tall, peaked, often elaborately decorated headdress of the BISHOP; also worn by the pope at LITURGICAL functions.

Monstrance A container used to display the CONSECRATED HOST for veneration.

Nave The wide central section between the entrance and the APSE of a BASILICA, usually flanked by side aisles, where the laity remains during the celebration of MASS.

Nunc Dimittis The Song of Simeon, its title deriving from the first two words of the Latin version, recited by Simeon during the Presentation of Christ in the Temple (Luke 2:29–32). As a CANTICLE, it is sung at CANDLEMAS.

Oblation The sacrifice of the EUCHARIST. The term is also applied to the material objects, the bread and wine, offered during this rite.

Offertory The worshipers' offering of the bread and wine to be used in the CONSECRATION, presented by the PRIEST on behalf of the congregation by the time of the Middle Ages. In the Early Christian period, the members of the congregation approached the ALTAR during the Offertory Procession, bringing gifts that sometimes included precious objects as well as bread and wine.

Officium Pastorum The Shepherds' Play, a medieval LITURGICAL drama performed on Christmas day, during which clergymen impersonating shepherds approached the ALTAR to adore an image of the Virgin and Child.

Officium Stellae The Play of the Magi, a medieval LITURGICAL drama performed at EPIPHANY, during which priests impersonating the Magi assembled at the high ALTAR and then followed a star to a second ALTAR, where they adored an image of the Virgin and Child.

Ordo Prophetarum A medieval LITURGICAL drama, immediately preceding the *OFFICIUM PASTORUM*, which consisted of a procession of prophets who quoted their own writings as announcements of the coming of Christ.

Paschal Referring to Passover. The Paschal lamb, originally the lamb eaten at Passover, signifies the SACRIFICIAL body of Christ.

Passion Derived from the Latin word that means to suffer, *passio*, the term designates the period of Christ's suffering from his entry into Jerusalem to his Crucifixion.

Paten The plate, usually circular

and often made of gold or silver, that holds the bread of the EUCHARIST on the ALTAR.

Pietà The Italian term for pity and piety. It refers to an image of the Virgin Mary lamenting the sacrificed body of Christ, who often lies across her lap.

Piscina A niche in a medieval church wall, usually located on the south side of the ALTAR, where the PRIEST washed his hands before and after MASS.

Polyptych A multipaneled ALTARPIECE, often with folding WINGS.

Praesepe (or *presepe*) The Latin term for crib or manger, used ambiguously in the texts of medieval LITURGICAL dramas to describe the structure on the ALTAR that held the image of the Virgin and Child.

Predella The low, oblong section of an ALTARPIECE below the main panel, more frequent in Italian painting than in the Netherlands. It is usually decorated with small figures or narrative scenes.

Prie-Dieu A French term meaning "pray God," designating a prayer desk for private use. Its top section consists of a support for a prayer book.

Priest A clergyman next in order below a BISHOP, who is ordained to celebrate MASS. The term "priesthood" refers to the office and characteristics of a priest.

Quem Queritis **Play** See VISITATIO SEPULCHRI.

Resurrection (of Christ) The miraculous rising of Christ from the tomb on the third day after his Crucifixion, celebrated by the Roman Catholic Church on EASTER Sunday.

Sacrament A term signifying the EUCHARIST alone or any of the other six rites ordained by Christ himself (i.e., BAPTISM, CONFIRMATION, Penance, HOLY ORDERS, Matrimony, and EXTREME UNC-

TION). Of the seven sacraments, Baptism and the Eucharist are the most essential for the achievement of SALVATION according to Catholic doctrine. The term "sacramental" refers to anything pertaining to a sacrament, especially to the Eucharist.

Sacrament House A monumental receptacle for the CONSECRATED HOST, usually shaped like a tower (see Fig. 20 here).

Sacramentary One of the oldest types of LITURGICAL book. Since it contained only the sections of MASS and other prayers recited by the CELEBRANT, it was gradually replaced by the more complete MISSAL.

Sacrifice (of the Mass) The OBLATION performed by the CELEBRANT at MASS that repeats the sacrifice of Christ on the cross. The term "sacrificial" refers to anything related to the EUCHARISTIC offering.

Salvation The redemption of mankind achieved through the death of Christ and the continual repetition of his SACRIFICE during MASS. According to Catholic thought, it can be attained only through BAPTISM and participation in the EUCHARISTIC rite.

Sanctuary The most sacred section of the church, containing the ALTAR.

Sepulchrum Literally, "sepulcher." A term used in texts of the *DEPOSITIO*, to describe the receptacle in which the CONSECRATED HOSTS were "buried" on GOOD FRIDAY.

Species The visible form of the Body and Blood of Christ as the CONSECRATED bread and wine of the EUCHARIST.

Stole A long, narrow LITURGICAL garment worn over the ALB. In the vestment of the DEACON, it is placed over the shoulder, with the ends tied together under the right arm.

Tabernacle Any receptacle used

to house the CONSECRATED HOST. For its shapes, see especially Chapter I, p. 32.

Tiara (papal) The elaborate triple crown worn by the pope at non-LITURGICAL ceremonial functions. It is usually surmounted by an orb and a cross, to designate the pope's supreme power (see Fig. 72 here).

Transubstantiation According to Catholic belief, the miraculous transformation of the bread and wine of the EUCHARIST into the Body and Blood of Christ, during the CONSECRATION.

Triptych A three-paneled ALTARPIECE, often hinged so that the narrower side WINGS can fold over the wider center panel.

Vespers The evening service of the Catholic Church, traditionally held at 6 PM or sunset. It is the sixth of the seven canonical hours for the recitation of prayers.

Visitatio Sepulchri The Visit of the Three Maries to the Tomb, one of the oldest LITURGICAL dramas, was performed during the Middle Ages on EASTER morning. Its alternate title, the *QUEM QUERITIS* play, derives from the initial question of the angel, "Whom are you seeking . . . ?" During this ceremony, clergymen impersonating the holy women approached the ALTAR, where a PRIEST dressed as an angel told them of Christ's RESURRECTION.

Wafer The thin piece of unleavened bread used in the EUCHARISTIC rite.

Wing A side panel of an ALTARPIECE, often hinged to the adjacent section in order to fold over it.

Brief Biographies of Early Netherlandish Artists

HIERONYMUS BOSCH (c. 1450–1516)
The name of this enigmatic Dutch painter derives from his birthplace, 's Hertogenbosch. Documents from this town in southern Holland mention him from 1486 until the year of his death. The altarpieces that he made for the cathedral there all seem to be lost, and no dated work by him remains. Although many paintings bear his name, the attribution of some of them and their chronological arrangement are still highly controversial. Most problematic of all is the interpretation of Bosch's tantalizing images, with their frightening and satirical combinations of animal, human, and inorganic forms. Scholars still debate the meanings of these fantastic creations, whose varied sources include late medieval proverbs, mysticism, alchemy, astronomy, and sorcery. References: Friedländer, V; Tolnay; Gibson; and, most recently, W. S. Gibson, *Hieronymus Bosch: an Annotated Bibliography,* Boston, 1983.

DIRC BOUTS (c. 1415–1475) Variously known as Dieric, Dirk, or Thierry. Bouts was born in Haarlem, where he may have studied with Ouwater before moving to Flanders. He settled in Louvain in 1457 and became its official painter in 1468. Extensive documentation survives for some of his major works, which portray profoundly symbolic ritualistic scenes in settings that reveal a strong concern with rational space. A similar interest in the works of Petrus Christus raises the controversial question of the exact connection between these two artists. Some scholars believe they may have trained together in Ouwater's workshop in Haarlem, whereas others suggest that Bouts worked with Christus in Bruges before he became established in Louvain. References: Friedländer, III; W. Schöne, *Dieric Bouts und seine Schule,* Berlin, 1938; Panofsky, 314ff.

ROBERT CAMPIN (c. 1378–1444) Documents in the Tournai archives refer to Robert Campin as a free master in 1406 and dean of the painters' guild in 1423. Since no signed panels by him remain, however, his style is still problematic. In 1427, Jacquelotte Daret and Rogelet de le Pasture became his apprentices. The close resemblance between four preserved panels of 1434 by Daret and some of the works attributed to the "Master of Flémalle" has led to the assumption that the latter artist must have been the teacher of Daret. Because the records tell us that Daret's teacher was none other than Campin, it follows that Campin must be the creator of the "Flémalle" paintings. Additional support

151

for this theory occurs in the similarities between the "Flémalle" works and the paintings by Rogier van der Weyden, who is usually recognized as the other apprentice of 1427, Rogelet de le Pasture. The "Flémalle" question is, however, still highly controversial.

References: Friedländer, II; Panofsky, 154ff.; Frinta; Davies; and, most recently, P. H. Schabacker, "Notes on the Biography of Robert Campin," *Mededelingen van de Koninklijke Academie voor Wetenschappen, Letteren en Schone Kunsten van België, Klasse der Schone Kunsten,* XLI, #2, 1980, 1ff.

PETRUS CHRISTUS (d. 1472 or 1473) First recorded as a citizen in Bruges in 1444, Christus remained its leading painter until his death. Although scholars have traditionally considered him a student of Van Eyck, there is no evidence that he was even in Bruges before Jan's death in 1441. His rich colors, elaboration of specific detail, and textural differentiation, however, reveal Jan's influence, as does his manner of signing and dating his paintings on the frame. Although he often quoted Van Eyck's compositional and iconographic motifs, his works also display remarkably original interpretations of traditional subjects. Christus may be identical with the "Piero di Bruges" who is recorded at Milan in 1456. Although his rational use of space may indicate an Italian influence, a similar concern appears in the works of his contemporary in Louvain, Dirc Bouts. This fascination with space is only one of a number of tantalizing parallels between these two artists. Christus' birthplace in Baerle, in the northern Netherlands, has suggested to some scholars that he may even have trained with Bouts in Ouwater's studio in Haarlem before going to Bruges.

References: Friedländer, I; Panofsky, 308ff.; Upton; P. H. Schabacker, *Petrus Christus,* Utrecht, 1974.

JACQUES DARET (active 1418–1473)

Mentioned as a member of Robert Campin's household as early as 1418, Jacques Daret is recorded as his apprentice in 1427. In 1432, this native of Tournai became both a master painter and the dean of the painters' guild. The only four panels that can definitely be attributed to him are now scattered among several museums, but once belonged to an altarpiece executed in 1434. Since they bear a close resemblance to the paintings attributed to the "Master of Flémalle," scholars have assumed that the latter artist must be none other than Daret's teacher, Robert Campin. Daret's works, therefore, are often cited in support of the identification of Campin with the "Flémalle" master.

References: M. Houtart, *Jacques Daret,* Tournai, 1908; Friedländer, II, 34ff.; Panofsky, 155ff.

GERARD DAVID (c. 1460–1523) In 1484, Gerard David became a member of the painters' guild of Bruges. There, he executed a number of commissions for the city government, and succeeded Memling as the city's leading painter. Because his works are similar in some respects to those of Geertgen tot Sint Jans, scholars have suggested that he trained in Ouwater's workshop in Haarlem. The fact that he was born in the northern Netherlands, near Gouda, lends support to this theory. David's rich, glowing colors and meticulous attention to detail recall the works of Jan van Eyck and Rogier van der Weyden, as do many of his compositional and iconographical motifs. His simple figure types and straightforward method of presentation, however, are closer to the works of Geertgen, and his most moving paintings possess a characteristic quiet tenderness and profound spirituality.

References: E. von Bodenhausen, *Gerard David und seine Schule,* Munich, 1905; Friedländer, VIb.

JAN VAN EYCK (d. 1441) Although we know that Jan van Eyck died in Bruges in 1441, we have no documents regarding the date or place of his birth. From 1422 to 1424, he worked for John of Bavaria, Count of Holland, at the palace of the Hague. After John's death in 1425, he became the court painter of Duke Philip the Good of Burgundy, in whose service he remained for the rest of his life. His exalted position in the Burgundian court gained him many favors from the Duke, for whom he made numerous distant and secret journeys. Nine of Jan's extant paintings are signed and dated. Of these, the earliest is the monumental Ghent Altarpiece of 1432 (Figs. 89 and 91), one of the most controversial works of the entire period. The damaged inscription on the lower frames of its exterior panels states that it was begun by Hubert van Eyck, the alleged brother of Jan. No other documented works by Hubert remain, however, and his contribution to the Ghent Altarpiece and relationship to Jan are still uncertain. Equally problematic is the character of the youthful production of Jan himself, since it is clear that he was already a mature artist by the time he produced the Ghent Altarpiece. There is no controversy, however, regarding his place as one of the founders of early Netherlandish painting. Although he did not actually invent oil painting, as Vasari claimed in his *Lives of the Painters* of 1550, his new sophisticated use of the oil medium enabled him to create colors of unprecedented depth and harmony. This intensity of color, as well as his rendering of specific detail, textural differentiation, and observation of light, contributed to the astounding naturalism of his spaces. Jan's tendency to endow every object in his pictures with profound symbolic significance laid the foundation for the complex levels of meaning that characterize the works of the whole fifteenth century in the Netherlands.

References: Friedländer, I; Baldass; Panofsky, especially 178ff.; Philip; Dhanens; and Snyder, "Chronology."

GEERTGEN TOT SINT JANS (d. c. 1495) No documentation remains for any work by this tantalizing Dutch painter. Most of our information about him derives from Van Mander's account in his *Dutch and Flemish Painters* of 1604. Van Mander wrote that Geertgen was born in Leyden, which he left to train in the workshop of Albrecht van Ouwater in Haarlem. Scholars often cite Geertgen's observant landscapes in support of this claim, since Van Mander praised Ouwater's excellence in landscape painting. In Haarlem, Geertgen lived in the monastery of the Order of Saint John, for which he produced many of his innovative compositions. His doll-like figures possess a wide-eyed innocence that conveys a profound sincerity. The intensely personal spirituality of his images parallels the mood of the *Devotio Moderna,* the Dutch movement that encouraged private contemplation.

References: Friedländer, V; Panofsky, 324ff.; Snyder.

HUGO VAN DER GOES (c. 1440–1482) Hugo is recorded as a master of the painters' guild in Ghent in 1467, and as its dean in 1474. He entered a monastery outside of Brussels in 1475, and remained there as a lay brother until his death. His biographer, the monk Gaspar Ofhuys, wrote that he experienced a suicidal mania caused by his feelings of inferiority to Jan van Eyck. When he died one year later, in 1482, he was still apparently unaware of the extraordinary originality of his achievement. The absence of any signed or dated painting by Hugo makes his stylistic progression extremely difficult to trace. In most of the intensely emotional works attributed to him, however, there is a new interest in the psychological reactions of the figures. The symbolism in these scenes is no less complex than in the paintings of the first half of the century, and their attention to detail and rich color recall the style of Van Eyck himself.

References: Friedländer, IV; Panofsky, 330ff.; Thompson and Campbell.

JOOS VAN GHENT (active c. 1460–1475) Variously known as Justus of Ghent, Joos van Gent, or Giusto da Guanto. Joos van Wassenhove, as he is called in the Flemish documents, joined the painters' guild in Antwerp in 1460. Four years later, he is recorded as a member of the guild in Ghent, where he sponsored the admission of Hugo van der Goes in 1467. After 1469, there is no record of him in Ghent. Documents from 1472 to 1475 record his activity in Urbino, where he worked for Duke Federigo da Montefeltro. Scholars have attributed a number of works to him on the basis of their similarity to his only extant documented painting, the monumental *Communion of the Apostles* (Fig. 75), which he executed for the Confraternity of Corpus Domini of Urbino in 1473 to 1474. His early works reflect the paintings of Dirc Bouts and Hugo van der Goes, especially in their interest in space, but they also possess a freer and less detailed painting style. In his later years, his forms became even more generalized, perhaps as a result of the influence of Italian painting.

References: Friedländer, III; J. Lavalleye, *Juste de Gand, peintre de Fédéric de Montefeltre,* Rome, 1936; Panofsky, 340ff.

MASTER OF FLÉMALLE This name was invented to denote the artist of three large panels, now in the Städelsches Kunstinstitut in Frankfurt (Friedländer, II, #60), which were alleged to have come from an abbey at Flémalle. Al-

though scholars eventually proved that no such abbey ever existed, the name continued to be applied to the body of work that had been grouped around these panels. Today, most scholars attribute this body of work to Robert Campin, although some writers still insist that the "Flémalle" paintings are actually youthful productions of Rogier van der Weyden. Writers agree, however, that this artist was working in the oil medium at least as early as Jan van Eyck. Whereas his pictures portray more humble figures in simpler, less rational spaces than in Jan's elegant settings, they are also remarkable for their brilliant color and complex symbolism.

References: Friedländer, II; Panofsky, especially 149ff.; Davies.

HANS MEMLING (c. 1440–1494) Memling was born near Frankfurt, in Seligenstadt-am-Main, but there are no records regarding his training in Germany before he left for Flanders. Vasari's reference to him as Rogier van der Weyden's pupil, in his frequently inaccurate *Lives of the Painters,* led to the assumption that he must have worked in Rogier's studio in Brussels from about 1459 or 1460 until Rogier's death in 1464. Memling's quotations of Rogierian motifs, in fact, prove no actual participation in Rogier's workshop, and no documents record that he was ever in Brussels at all. We do know, however, that he became a citizen of Bruges in 1465, entered its painters' guild in 1467, and soon became its leading painter. By the time of his death, he was one of the city's wealthiest citizens, having achieved fame in England, Spain, Italy, and Germany, as well as in Flanders itself. His characteristic brilliant color and technical perfection appear in a number of major works that he executed for Saint John's Hospital in Bruges, where they are still preserved in almost their original splendor. The calm figures of Memling's paintings convey a quiet mysticism that contrasts dramatically with the tormented creations of his exact contemporary in Ghent, Hugo van der Goes. His interest in narrative detail distinguishes him from his predecessors, and his ability to capture the individuality of his patrons explains why he was the most successful portraitist of the period.

References: Friedländer, VIa and b; L. von Baldass, *Hans Memling,* Vienna, 1942; K. B. McFarlane, *Hans Memling,* Oxford, 1971; Lane, *Memling.*

ALBERT VAN OUWATER (active c. 1450–1475) In his *Dutch and Flemish Painters* of 1604, Van Mander wrote that Ouwater was the head of the Haarlem school of painting. Although Van Mander extolled him as a master of landscapes, Ouwater's only firmly attributed extant panel is an interior scene: the *Raising of Lazarus* in the Staatliche Museen in Berlin. Because the style of this painting recalls Christus and Bouts, scholars argue about the exact connection between these three artists. Whereas some writers insist that Ouwater trained with Christus in Bruges, others suggest that both Christus and Bouts began in Ouwater's shop in Haarlem. There are, in fact, no less than nine possibilities for explaining this relationship, as Snyder has noted. The association of Geertgen tot Sint Jans with Ouwater is also problematic, although Van Mander described him as Ouwater's pupil.

References: Friedländer, III, 34ff.; Panofsky, 319ff.; J. E. Snyder, "The Early Haarlem School of Painting, I: Ouwater and the Master of the Tiburtine Sibyl," *Art Bulletin,* XLII, 1960, 39ff.

ROGIER VAN DER WEYDEN (1399/1400–1464) Also known as Roger de le Pasture. In 1435, Rogier van der Weyden became the official painter of Brussels. At his death there in 1464, the painters' guild held a special Mass in his honor. Although his fame as the leading painter of Brussels between these years is indisputable, his origins remain obscure. The controversy over his early training is partly a result of nationalistic concerns. For years, scholars from the Flemish part of Belgium insisted that he was a student of Van Eyck in Bruges, and identified him with the "Rogier of Bruges" mentioned in the documents. French writers, on the other hand, defended the theory that he trained in Tournai under Robert Campin, and accepted him as the "Rogelet de le Pasture" who became Campin's apprentice in 1427. Today, most scholars lean toward the latter alternative, and recognize his birthplace as Tournai as well. Because we have no signed or dated paintings by Rogier, the body of work attributed to him is also highly controversial. A few writers still believe in the theory that the panels ascribed to the so-called "Master of Flémalle" should be recognized as Rogier's youthful productions. Some of his accepted paintings are, in fact, remarkably close in style to the "Flémalle" works, and their chronological arrangement is still extremely problematic. Rogier invented many compositional types that became the models for generations of Flemish painters. The lyrical rhythms of his flowing line and his gentle, profound emotionality endeared him to his contemporaries and followers. His paintings contain complex theological meanings that are often expressed by innovative compositional motifs. Rogier was undoubtedly the most influential Netherlandish painter of the fifteenth century, but his grace and tenderness were never equaled.

References: Friedländer, II; Panofsky, 247ff.; T. H. Feder, "A Reexamination Through Documents of the First Fifty Years of Roger van der Weyden's Life," *Art Bulletin,* XLVIII, 1966, 416ff.; Davies.

Selected Bibliography

An item listed in the bibliography is referred to in the footnotes only by the author's name, unless further information is needed to distinguish the publication from others by the same author. Works listed only once in the footnotes appear in the bibliography only if they relate specifically to the subject of this study.

Amadeus of Lausanne. *Huit homélies mariales,* ed. G. Vabaud (Sources Chrétiennes, no. 72). Paris, 1960.

Baldass, Ludwig von. *Jan van Eyck.* London, 1952.

Barthélemy, Charles, trans. *Rational ou manuel des divins offices de Guillaume Durand,* 5 vols. Paris, 1854.

Baumer, Christoph. "Die Schreinmadonna," *Marian Library Studies,* IX, 1977, 239–272.

Benjamin, Lloyd. "Disguised Symbolism Exposed and the History of Early Netherlandish Painting," *Studies in Iconography,* II, 1976, 11–24.

Berlin, Staatliche Museen. *Beschreibendes Verzeichnis der Gemälde im Kaiser-Friedrich Museum und Deutschen Museum.* Berlin, 1931.

Bernard of Clairvaux and Amadeus of Lausanne. *Magnificat. Homilies in Praise of the Blessed Virgin Mary,* trans. M.-B. Saïd and G. Perigo (Cistercian Fathers Series, no. 18). Kalamazoo, 1979.

Birkmeyer, Karl M. "The Arch Motif in Netherlandish Painting of the Fifteenth Century," *Art Bulletin,* XLIII, 1961, 1–20, 99–112.

Blum, Shirley Neilsen. *Early Netherlandish Triptychs: a Study in Patronage.* Berkeley and Los Angeles, 1969. Referred to in the notes as "Blum."

———. "Symbolic Invention in the Art of Rogier van der Weyden," *Konsthistorisk Tidscrift,* XLVI, 1977, 103–122. Referred to in the notes as "Blum, 'Symbolic Invention.' "

Bodenstedt, Mary Immaculate. *The Vita Christi of Ludolphus the Carthusian* (The Catholic University of America Studies in Latin Language and Literature, XVI). Washington, D. C., 1944.

Boom, Gh. de. "Le Culte de l'Eucharistie d'après la miniature du moyen âge," in *Studia Eucharistica,* Antwerp, 1946, 326–332.

Borchgrave d'Altena, J. de. "Madones en majesté, à propos de Notre Dame d'Eprave," *Revue belge d'archéologie et d'historie de l'art,* XXX, 1961, 3–114.

Bourassé, J. J. *Summa Aurea de Laudibus Beatissimae Virginis Mariae,* III. Paris, 1866.

Braun, Joseph. *Der christliche Altar in seiner geschichtlichen Entwicklung,* 2 vols. Munich, 1924.

Breitenbach, Edgar. *Speculum Humanae Salvationis, eine typengeschichtliche Untersuchung.* Strassburg, 1930.

Brooks, Neil C. *The Sepulchre of Christ in Art and Liturgy, with Special Reference to the Liturgic Drama* (University of Illinois Studies in Language and Literature, VII, no. 2), Urbana, 1921, 141–248.

Browe, Peter. *Die eucharistischen Wunder des Mittelalters.* Breslau, 1938. Referred to in the notes as "Browe, *Eucharistischen Wunder.*"

———. *Die Verehrung der Eucharistie im Mittelalter.* Reprint of the 1932 ed. Rome, 1967. Referred to in the notes as "Browe, *Verehrung der Eucharistie.*"

Capizzi, Carmelo. *Pantocrator* (Orientalia Christiana Analecta, 170). Rome, 1964.

Caspary, Hans. *Das Sakramentstabernakel in Italien bis zum Konzil von Trient.* Munich, 1965.

Cohen, Gustave. *Le Théatre française en Belgique au moyen âge.* Brussels, 1953.

Cornell, Henrik. *Biblia Pauperum.* Stockholm, 1925. Referred to in the notes as "Cornell."

———. *The Iconography of the Nativity of Christ.* Uppsala, 1924. Referred to in the notes as "Cornell, *Iconography.*"

Cuttler, Charles D. *Northern Painting from Pucelle to Bruegel.* New York, 1968.

Davies, Martin. *National Gallery Catalogues: Early Netherlandish School,* 3rd ed. London, 1968. Referred to in the notes as "Davies, *Early Netherlandish School.*"

———. *The National Gallery, London, I* (Les Primitifs Flamands, III). Antwerp, 1953. Referred to in the notes as "Davies, *National Gallery.*"

———. *Rogier van der Weyden.* London, 1972. Referred to in the notes as "Davies."

Delaissé, L. M. J. *A Century of Dutch Manuscript Illumination.* Berkeley and Los Angeles, 1968.

Dhanens, Elisabeth. *Van Eyck: The Ghent Altarpiece* (Art in Context). New York, 1973.

Dobrzeniecki, Tadeusz. "Medieval Sources of the Pietà," *Bulletin du Musée National de Varsovie,* VIII, 1967, 5–24.

Dumoutet, Edouard. *Le Désir de voir l'Hostie et les origins de la dévotion au Saint-Sacrement.* Paris, 1926.

Dupont, Jacques. "Le Sacerdoce de la Vierge: Le Puy d'Amiens en 1437," *Gazette des beaux-arts,* ser. 6, VIII, 1932, 265–74.

Eisler, Colin. "The Golden Christ of Cortona and the Man of Sorrows in Italy," *Art Bulletin,* LI, 1969, 107–18, 233–46.

Forsyth, Ilene H. "Magi and Majesty: a Study of Romanesque Sculpture and Liturgical Drama," *Art Bulletin,* L, 1968, 215–22. Referred to in the notes as "Forsyth, 'Magi.'"

———. *The Throne of Wisdom.* Princeton, 1972. Referred to in the notes as "Forsyth, *Throne.*"

Forsyth, William H. *The Entombment of Christ: French Sculptures of the Fifteenth and Sixteenth Centuries.* Cambridge, Mass., 1970. Referred to in the notes as "Forsyth, *Entombment.*"

Freestone, William Herbert. *The Sacrament Reserved.* London, 1917.

Friedländer, Max J. *Early Netherlandish*

Painting, trans. Heinz Norden from the German edition of 1924–37; 14 vols. Leyden, New York, and Washington, 1967–76.

Fries, Walter. "Die Schreinmadonna," *Anzeiger des Germanischen Nationalmuseums,* Nuremberg, 1928–29, 5–69.

Frinta, Mojmir S. *The Genius of Robert Campin.* Paris, 1966.

Gibson, Walter S. *Hieronymus Bosch.* New York and Washington, 1973.

Gilbert, Creighton E. "Last Suppers and Their Refectories," in *The Pursuit of Holiness in Late Medieval and Renaissance Religion,* ed. C. Trinkaus, Leyden, 1974, 371–402.

Gottlieb, Carla. "'En ipse stat post parietem nostrum': the Symbolism of the Ghent 'Annunciation,'" *Bulletin des Musées Royaux des Beaux-Arts de Belgique,* XIX, 1970, 75–97. Referred to in the notes as "Gottlieb, 'En ipse stat post parietem nostrum.'"

———. "The Living Host," *Konsthistorisk Tidskrift,* XL, 1971, 30–46. Referred to in the notes as "Gottlieb, 'Living Host.'"

———. "The Mystical Window in Paintings of the Salvator Mundi," *Gazette des beaux-arts,* ser. 6, LVI, 1960, 313–32. Referred to in the notes as "Gottlieb, 'Mystical Window.'"

———. "Respiciens per Fenestras: the Symbolism of the Mérode Altarpiece," *Oud-Holland,* LXXXV, 1970, 65–84. Referred to in the notes as "Gottlieb."

Grosshans, Rainald. "Rogier van der Weyden. Der Marienaltar aus der Kartause Miraflores," *Jahrbuch der Berliner Museen,* XXIII, 1981, 49–112.

Guarducci, Margherita. "Ara Caeli," in *Atti della Pontificia Accademia Romana di Archeologia, Rendiconti,* XXIII–XXIV, 1947–49, 279–90.

Hagar, Hellmut. *Die Anfänge des italienischen Altarbildes.* Munich, 1962.

Harbison, Craig. "Some Artistic Anticipations of Theological Thought," *Art Quarterly,* II, 1979, 67–89.

Hardison, O. B. *Christian Rite and Christian Drama in the Middle Ages.* Baltimore, 1965.

Held, Julius S. Review of *Early Netherlandish Painting* by Erwin Panofsky, *Art Bulletin,* XXXVII, 1955, 205–34.

Hirn, Yrjö. *The Sacred Shrine, a Study of the Poetry and Art of the Catholic Church,* trans. from the Swedish edition of 1909; 2nd English ed. Boston, 1957.

Hulin de Loo, Georges. *Heures de Milan.* Paris, 1911.

Hull, Vida Joyce. *Hans Memlinc's Paintings for the Hospital of Saint John in Bruges* (Ph.D. dissertation, Bryn Mawr College, 1979). New York, 1981.

Jungmann, Joseph A. *The Mass.* Collegeville, 1976. Referred to in the notes as "Jungmann, *Mass.*"

———. *The Mass of the Roman Rite: Its Origins and Development,* trans. F. A. Brunner from the German edition of 1949; 2 vols. New York, 1951. Referred to in the notes as "Jungmann."

Katzenellenbogen, Adolf. *The Sculptural Programs of Chartres Cathedral.* Reprint of the 1959 edition. New York, 1964.

Kidd, B. J. *The Later Medieval Doctrine of the Eucharistic Sacrifice.* London, 1898.

King, Archdale A. *Eucharistic Reservation in the Western Church.* London, 1965.

Koch, Robert A. "Flower Symbolism in the Portinari Altar," *Art Bulletin,* XLVI, 1964, 70–77.

Lane, Barbara G. "'Depositio et Elevatio': the Symbolism of the Seilern Triptych," *Art Bulletin,* LVII, 1975, 21–30. Referred to in the notes as "Lane, 'Depositio et Elevatio.'"

————. "Early Italian Sources for the Braque Triptych," *Art Bulletin,* LXII, 1980, 281–84. Referred to in the notes as "Lane, 'Early Italian Sources.' "

————. " 'Ecce Panis Angelorum': the Manger as Altar in Hugo's Berlin Nativity," *Art Bulletin,* LVII, 1975, 476–86. Referred to in the notes as "Lane, 'Ecce Panis Angelorum.' "

————. *Hans Memling* (Die grossen Meister der Malerei). Frankfurt am Main, 1980. Referred to in the notes as "Lane, *Memling.*"

————. "Petrus Christus: a Reconstructed Triptych with an Italian Motif," *Art Bulletin,* LII, 1970, 390–93. Referred to in the notes as "Lane, 'Petrus Christus.' "

————. "Rogier's Saint John and Miraflores Altarpieces Reconsidered," *Art Bulletin,* LX, 1978, 655–72. Referred to in the notes as "Lane, 'Rogier's Altarpieces.' "

————. "The 'Symbolic Crucifixion' in the Hours of Catherine of Cleves," *Oud-Holland,* LXXXVI, 1973, 4–26. Referred to in the notes as "Lane, 'Symbolic Crucifixion.' "

Laurentin, René. "Digne vesture au prestre souverain," *Revue du moyen âge latin,* IV, 1948, 253–74. Referred to in the notes as "Laurentin, 'Digne vesture.' "

————. *Maria, Ecclesia, Sacerdotium. Essai sur le développement d'une idée religieuse* (Ph.D. dissertation, University of Paris, 1952). Paris, 1952. Referred to in the notes as "Laurentin."

Lavin, Marilyn Aronberg. "The Altar of Corpus Domini in Urbino: Paolo Uccello, Joos van Ghent, Piero della Francesca," *Art Bulletin,* XLIX, 1967, 1–24.

Leprieur, Paul. "Un triptyque de Roger de la Pasture au Musée du Louvre," *Gazette des beaux-arts,* ser. 4, X, 1913, 257–80.

Lexikon der christliche Ikonographie, ed. E. Kirschbaum et al., 8 vols. Freiburg im Breisgau, 1968–76. Referred to in the notes as "*Lexikon.*"

Loomis, Laura Hibbard. "The Table of the Last Supper in Religious and Secular Iconography," *Art Studies,* V, 1927, 71–88.

Ludolphus de Saxonia. *Vita Jesu Christi,* ed. L. M. Rigollot, 4 vols., 2nd edition. Paris and Brussels, 1878.

Lutz, J., and Perdrizet, P. *Speculum Humanae Salvationis,* 2 vols. Mulhouse, 1907–09.

Maffei, E. *La Réservation eucharistique jusqu'à la Renaissance.* Brussels, 1942.

Mâle, Emile. *L'Art religieux de la fin du moyen âge en France,* 4th edition. Paris, 1931. Referred to in the notes as "Mâle."

————. *Religious Art in France: the Twelfth Century,* trans. from the 1953 French edition. Princeton, 1978. Referred to in the notes as "Mâle, *Religious Art.*"

————. "Les Rois mages et le drame liturgique," *Gazette des beaux-arts,* ser. 4, IV, 1910, 261–70. Referred to in the notes as "Mâle, 'Les Rois mages.' "

McNamee, M. B. "An Additional Eucharistic Allusion in Van der Weyden's 'Columba Triptych,' " *Studies in Iconography,* II, 1976, 107–13. Referred to in the notes as "McNamee, 'Additional Eucharistic Allusion.' "

————. "Further Symbolism in the Portinari Altarpiece," *Art Bulletin,* XLV, 1963, 142–43. Referred to in the notes as "McNamee, 'Further Symbolism.' "

————. "The Good Friday Liturgy and Hans Memling's Antwerp Triptych," *Journal of the Warburg and Courtauld Institutes,* XXXVII, 1974, 353–56. Referred to in the notes as "McNamee, 'Good Friday Liturgy.' "

————. "The Medieval Latin Liturgical

Drama and the Annunciation Triptych of the Master of the Aix-en-Provence Annunciation," *Gazette des beaux-arts,* ser. 6, LXXXIII, 1974, 37–40. Referred to in the notes as "McNamee, 'Drama.' "

———. "The Origin of the Vested Angel as a Eucharistic Symbol in Flemish Painting," *Art Bulletin,* LIV, 1972, 263–78. Referred to in the notes as "McNamee, 'Origin of the Vested Angel.' "

Meiss, Millard. *French Painting in the Time of Jean de Berry: the Late Fourteenth Century and the Patronage of the Duke,* 2 vols. London and New York, 1967. Referred to in the notes as "Meiss."

———. *French Painting in the Time of Jean de Berry: the Limbourgs and their Contemporaries,* 2 vols. New York, 1974. Referred to in the notes as "Meiss, *Limbourgs.*"

———. "The Madonna of Humility," *Art Bulletin,* XVIII, 1936, 435–464. Referred to in the notes as "Meiss, 'Madonna of Humility.' "

———. *Painting in Florence and Siena after the Black Death.* Reprint of the 1951 edition. New York, 1964. Referred to in the notes as "Meiss, *Painting in Florence and Siena.*"

Migne, J. P., ed. *Patrologiae Cursus Completus . . . Series Graeca,* 162 vols. Paris, 1857–1912. Referred to in the notes as "Migne, *P.G.*"

———. *Patrologiae Cursus Completus . . . Series Latina,* 221 vols. Paris, 1844–64. Referred to in the notes as "Migne, *P.L.*"

Millet, Gabriel. *Recherches sur l'iconographie de l'Evangile.* Paris, 1916.

Minott, Charles Ilsley. "The Theme of the Mérode Altarpiece," *Art Bulletin,* LI, 1969, 267–71.

Mone, Franz Joseph. *Lateinische Hymnen des Mittelalters, II: Marienlieder.* Reprint of the 1854 edition. Darmstadt, 1964.

Neale, John Mason, and Webb, Benjamin, trans. *The Symbolism of Churches and Church Ornaments, a Translation of the First Book of the Rationale Divinorum Officiorum Written by William Durandus.* New York, 1893.

Nilgen, Ursula. "The Epiphany and the Eucharist: On the Interpretation of Eucharistic Motifs in Mediaeval Epiphany Scenes," *Art Bulletin,* XLIX, 1967, 311–16.

O'Meara, Carra Ferguson. "'In the Hearth of the Virginal Womb': the Iconography of the Holocaust in Late Medieval Art," *Art Bulletin,* LXIII, 1981, 75–88.

Oxford Dictionary of the Christian Church, ed. F. L. Cross and E. A. Livingstone, 2nd ed. Oxford, 1974. Referred to in the notes as "*Oxford Dictionary.*"

Panofsky, Erwin. *Early Netherlandish Painting: Its Origins and Character,* 2 vols. Cambridge, Mass., 1953. Referred to in the notes as "Panofsky."

———. "'Imago Pietatis,' Ein Beitrag zur Typengeschichte des 'Schmerzensmanns' und der 'Maria Mediatrix,'" in *Festschrift für Max J. Friedländer zum 60. Geburtstage,* Leipzig, 1927, 261–308. Referred to in the notes as "Panofsky, 'Imago Pietatis.'"

Parker, Elizabeth C. *The Descent from the Cross: Its Relation to the Extra-Liturgical 'Depositio' Drama* (Ph.D. dissertation, New York University, 1975). New York, 1978.

Parshall, Peter W. Review of *Early Netherlandish Triptychs* by Shirley Neilson Blum, *Burlington Magazine,* CXIV, 1972, 247–48.

Philip, Lotte Brand. *The Ghent Altarpiece and the Art of Jan van Eyck.* Princeton, 1971. Referred to in the notes as "Philip."

———. "Eine kölnische Kreuzigung im Historischen Museum Basel," *Wallraf-Richartz-Jahrbuch,* XXI, 1959,

223–26. Referred to in the Notes as "Philip, 'Kölnische Kreuzigung.'"

———. "The Prado Epiphany by Jerome Bosch," *Art Bulletin*, XXXV, 1953, 267–93. Referred to in the notes as "Philip, 'Prado Epiphany.'"

Plummer, John. *Liturgical Manuscripts for the Mass and the Divine Office*. New York, 1964.

Pugin, A. Welby. *Glossary of Ecclesiastical Ornament and Costume*, 3rd ed. London, 1868.

Purtle, Carol J. *The Marian Paintings of Jan van Eyck*. Princeton, 1982.

Ragusa, Isa, and Green, Rosalie B., ed. *Meditations on the Life of Christ*. Princeton, 1961.

Raible, Felix. *Der Tabernakel einst und jetzt. Eine historische und liturgische Darstellung der Andacht zur aufbewahrten Eucharistie*. Freiburg im Breisgau, 1908.

Réau, Louis. *Iconographie de l'art chrétien*, 6 vols. Paris, 1955–59.

Reusens, E. *Eléments d'archéologie chrétienne*, 2 vols. Louvain, 1875.

Ring, Grete. *A Century of French Painting, 1400–1500*. Reprint of the 1949 edition. New York, 1979.

Ringbom, Sixten. *Icon to Narrative. The Rise of the Dramatic Close-up in Fifteenth-Century Devotional Painting*. Åbo, 1965.

Robb, David M. "The Iconography of the Annunciation in the Fourteenth and Fifteenth Centuries," *Art Bulletin*, XVIII, 1936, 480–526.

Roman Missal in Latin and English. New York: Benziger Brothers, 1910. Referred to in the notes as "*Roman Missal*."

Schapiro, Meyer. "Two Romanesque Drawings in Auxerre and Some Iconographic Problems," in *Studies in Art and Literature for Belle da Costa Greene*, Princeton, 1954, 331–49.

Scheingorn, Pamela. "The Sepulchrum Domini: a Study in Art and Liturgy," *Studies in Iconography*, IV, 1978, 37–60.

Schiller, Gertrud. *Ikonographie der christlichen Kunst*, 4 vols. Gütersloh, 1966–76.

Schwarzweber, Annemarie. *Das heilige Grab in der deutschen Bildnerei des Mittelalters*. Freiburg im Breisgau, 1940.

Shorr, Dorothy C. "The Iconographic Development of the Presentation in the Temple," *Art Bulletin*, XXVIII, 1946, 17–32.

Sinanoglou, Leah. "The Christ Child as Sacrifice: a Medieval Tradition and the Corpus Christi Plays," *Speculum*, XLVIII, 1973, 491–509.

Smith, Molly Teasdale. "The Use of Grisaille as a Lenten Observance," *Marsyas*, VIII, 1957–59, 43–54.

Snyder, James. "The Chronology of Jan van Eyck's Paintings," in *Album Amicorum J. G. van Gelder*, The Hague, 1973, 293–97. Referred to in the notes as "Snyder, 'Chronology.'"

———. "The Early Haarlem School of Painting: II. Geertgen tot Sint Jans," *Art Bulletin*, XLII, 1960, 113–32. Referred to in the notes as "Snyder."

———. "Jan van Eyck and the Madonna of Chancellor Nicolas Rolin," *Oud-Holland*, LXXXII, 1967, 163–71. Referred to in the notes as "Snyder, 'Jan van Eyck and the Madonna of Chancellor Nicolas Rolin.'"

Stange, Alfred. *Deutsche Malerei der Gothik*, 11 vols. Berlin, 1934–61.

Stubblebine, James H. "Segna di Buonaventura and the Image of the Man of Sorrows," *Gesta*, VIII, pt. 2, 1969, 3–13.

Tauler, Johann. *Oeuvres complètes. VI. Exercises ou méditations sur la vie et la Passion de Jésus-Christ*, ed. E.-P. Noël. Paris, 1912.

Thompson, Colin, and Campbell, Lorne. *Hugo van der Goes and the Trinity Panels in Edinburgh*. London, 1974.

Tolnay, Charles de. *Hieronymus Bosch.* Basle, 1937.

Upton, Joel M. "Devotional Imagery and Style in the Washington Nativity by Petrus Christus," *Studies in the History of Art* (Washington, National Gallery of Art), VII, 1975, 49–79. Referred to in the notes as "Upton, 'Devotional Imagery.'"

———. "Petrus Christus." Ph.D. dissertation, Bryn Mawr College, 1972. Referred to in the notes as "Upton."

Van Buren, Anne Hagopian. "The Canonical Office in Renaissance Painting, Part II: More About the Rolin Madonna," *Art Bulletin,* LX, 1978, 617–633.

Van Dijk, S. J. P., and Walker, J. Hazelden. *The Myth of the Aumbry. Notes on Medieval Reservation Practice and Eucharistic Devotion.* London, 1957.

Van Gelder, J. G. "An Early Work by Robert Campin," *Oud-Holland,* LXXXII, 1967, 1–17.

Van Mander, Carel. *Dutch and Flemish Painters,* trans. C. van de Wall from the Dutch edition of 1604. New York, 1936.

Van Marle, Raimond. *The Development of the Italian Schools of Painting,* 19 vols. The Hague, 1923–38.

Van Schoute, Roger. *La Chapelle Royal de Grenade* (Les Primitifs Flamands, VI). Brussels, 1963.

Veronee-Verhaegen, Nicole. *L'Hôtel-Dieu de Beaune* (Les Primitifs Flamands, XIII). Brussels, 1973.

Vloberg, Maurice. *L'Eucharistie dans l'art.* Grenoble and Paris, 1946.

Von Simson, Otto Georg. "*Compassio* and *Co-Redemptio* in Roger van der Weyden's Descent from the Cross," *Art Bulletin,* XXXV, 1953, 9–16. Referred to in the notes as "Von Simson."

———. *The Sacred Fortress. Byzantine Art and Statecraft in Ravenna.* Chicago, 1948. Referred to in the notes as "Von Simson, *Sacred Fortress.*"

Voragine, Jacobus da. *The Golden Legend,* trans. G. Ryan and H. Ripperger. Reprint of the 1941 edition. New York, 1969.

Warner, Marina. *Alone of All Her Sex. The Myth and the Cult of the Virgin Mary.* New York, 1976.

Young, Karl. *The Drama of the Medieval Church,* 2 vols. Oxford, 1933. Referred to in the notes as "Young."

———. *The Dramatic Associations of the Easter Sepulchre* (University of Wisconsin Studies in Language and Literature, no. 10). Madison, 1920. Referred to in the notes as "Young, *Dramatic Associations.*"

———. "Dramatic Ceremonies of the Feast of the Purification," *Speculum,* V, 1930, 97–102. Referred to in the notes as "Young, 'Dramatic Ceremonies.'"

———. "Officium Pastorum: a Study of the Dramatic Developments within the Liturgy of Christmas," *Transactions of the Wisconsin Academy of Sciences, Arts and Letters,* XVII, pt. 1, Madison, 1914, 299–396. Referred to in the notes as "Young, 'Officium Pastorum.'"

———. "Ordo Prophetarum," *Transactions of the Wisconsin Academy of Sciences, Arts, and Letters,* XX, Madison, 1921, 1–82. Referred to in the notes as "Young, 'Ordo Prophetarum.'"

List of Illustrations

York, Metropolitan Museum of Art, Gift of J. Pierpont Morgan, 1917.

18. *Vierge Ouvrante,* open. New York, Metropolitan Museum of Art, Gift of J. Pierpont Morgan, 1917.

19. Rogier van der Weyden, "Medici Madonna." Frankfurt, Städelsches Kunstinstitut (courtesy Städelsches Kunstinstitut).

20. Sacrament House. Louvain, Collegiate Church of St. Peter (copyright A.C.L. Brussels).

21. Hans Memling, *Madonna and Child with Angels.* Washington, D.C., National Gallery of Art, Andrew Mellon Collection.

22. Aumbry. Wenduyne (copyright A.C.L. Brussels).

23. Aumbry. Leefdael, Sainte Vérone (copyright A.C.L. Brussels).

24. Jan Provost. *Altarpiece of the Virgin Enthroned,* center panel. Lisbon, Museu Nacional de Arte Antiga.

25. Robert Campin, Mérode Altarpiece, center panel: *Annunciation.* New York, Metropolitan Museum of Art, The Cloisters Collection, Purchase.

26. *Priest Washing His Hands.* Utrecht, University Library, ms. 400, fol. 1r., detail (photo: University Library, Utrecht).

27. Master of Catherine of Cleves, *Annunciation, Hours of Katharina van Lochorst.* Münster, Westfälisches Landesmuseum für Kunst and Kulturgeschichte, ms. 530, fol. 16v. (courtesy Westfälisches Landesmuseum).

28. Jan van Eyck, *Annunciation.* Washington, D.C., National Gallery of Art, Andrew Mellon Collection.

29. Rogier van der Weyden, *Annunciation.* Paris, Musée du Louvre (Cliché des Musées Nationaux, Paris).

30. Rogier van der Weyden, Columba Altarpiece, left wing: *Annunciation.* Munich, Alte Pinakothek.

31. Hugo van der Goes, *Nativity.* Berlin, Staatliche Museen Preussischer Kulturbesitz, Gemäldegalerie.

32. *Nativity.* Munich, Bayerisches Nationalmuseum.

33. Hugo van der Goes, Portinari Altarpiece. Florence, Uffizi (photo: Gabinetto fotografico della Soprintendenza ai Beni Artistici e Storici di Firenze).

34. Gerard David, *Nativity with Donors and Patron Saints,* center panel: *Nativity.* New York, Metropolitan Museum of Art, Jules S. Bache Collection, 1949.

35. Master of Saint Giles, *Mass of Saint Giles.* London, The National Gallery (reproduced by courtesy of the Trustees, The National Gallery, London).

36. *Incarnation* Window, detail: *Nativity.* Chartres Cathedral (copyright Arch. Phot./SPADEM, Paris/VAGA, New York, 1982).

37. Petrus Christus, *Nativity.* Washington, D.C., National Gallery of Art, Andrew Mellon Collection.

38. Geertgen tot Sint Jans, *Nativity.* London, The National Gallery (reproduced by courtesy of the Trustees, The National Gallery, London).

39. Rogier van der Weyden, Columba Altarpiece. Munich, Alte Pinakothek.

40. Rogier van der Weyden, Columba Altarpiece, center panel: *Adoration of the Magi.* Munich, Alte Pinakothek.

41. Hans Memling, Altarpiece of the Adoration of the Magi, center panel: *Adoration of the Magi.* Madrid, Museo del Prado (copyright Museo del Prado).

42. Gerard David, *Adoration of the Magi.* London, The National Gallery (reproduced by courtesy of the Trustees, The National Gallery, London).

43. Hieronymus Bosch, *Epiphany* Triptych, interior. Madrid, Museo del Prado (copyright Museo del Prado).

44. Hieronymus Bosch, *Epiphany* Triptych, exterior: *Mass of Saint Gregory.* Madrid, Museo del Prado (copyright Museo del Prado).

139r. (Phot. Bibl. Nat. Paris).

71. *Christ Blessing the Wafer and Chalice.* New York, Pierpont Morgan Library, M. 331, fol. 156v. (Courtesy Pierpont Morgan Library).

72. Jan van Eyck, Ghent Altarpiece, detail of Figure 91: *Christ.* Ghent, St. Bavo (copyright A.C.L. Brussels).

73. Hans Memling, *Salvator Mundi with Singing Angels,* center panel. Antwerp, Koninklijk Museum (copyright A.C.L. Brussels; courtesy Koninklijk Museum).

74. *Last Supper, Heures de Milan.* Turin, Museo Civico, fol. 90r. (copyright Museo Civico di Torino).

75. Joos van Ghent, *Communion of the Apostles.* Urbino, Galleria Nazionale delle Marche (copyright A.C.L. Brussels).

76. *Communion of the Apostles, Très Riches Heures du Duc de Berry.* Chantilly, Musée Condé, ms. 65/1284, fol. 189v., detail (Photo Giraudon, Paris).

77. Rogier van der Weyden, Braque Triptych. Paris, Musée du Louvre (copyright A.C.L. Brussels; courtesy Musées Nationaux, Paris).

78. Cimabue and others, *Pantocrator.* Pisa Cathedral (photo: Alinari/Art Resource, Inc.).

79. *Christ in Majesty, Gospel Book of Lothair.* Paris, Bibliothèque Nationale, ms. lat. 266, fol. 2v. (Phot. Bibl. Nat. Paris).

80. *Christ in Majesty.* Zurich, Zentralbibliothek, Ms. C 80, fol. 83r. (courtesy Zentralbibliothek).

81. *John the Evangelist as Priest at His Last Mass, Apocalypse.* Manchester, John Rylands University Library, Rylands Latin Ms. 19, fol. 24v. (courtesy John Rylands University Library of Manchester, The University of Manchester).

82. Rogier van der Weyden, Braque Triptych, detail of Figure 77: *Mary Magdalen* (Cliché des Musées Nationaux, Paris).

83. Meliore Toscano, *Christ and Saints.* Florence, Uffizi (photo: Alinari/Art Resource, Inc.).

84. Pietro Nelli and Tommaso del Mazza, Predella with Christ as Man of Sorrows, center panel. Impruneta, Chiesa Collegiata (photo: Alinari/Art Resource, Inc.).

85. Tomb of Tedice Aliotti. Florence, Sta. Maria Novella (photo: Alinari/Art Resource, Inc.).

86. Geertgen tot Sint Jans, *Man of Sorrows.* Utrecht, Het Catharijneconvent (photo: Stichting Het Catharijneconvent).

87. Robert Campin, *Mass of Saint Gregory.* Brussels, Musées Royaux des Beaux-Arts de Belgique (copyright A.C.L. Brussels).

88. Petrus Christus, *Man of Sorrows.* Birmingham, England, City Museums and Art Gallery.

89. Jan van Eyck, Ghent Altarpiece, exterior. Ghent, St. Bavo (copyright A.C.L. Brussels).

90. Rogier van der Weyden, *Last Judgment* Altarpiece, exterior. Beaune, Hôtel-Dieu (copyright A.C.L. Brussels).

91. Jan van Eyck, Ghent Altarpiece, interior. Ghent, St. Bavo (copyright A.C.L. Brussels).

92. Rogier van der Weyden, *Last Judgment* Altarpiece, interior. Beaune, Hôtel-Dieu (copyright A.C.L. Brussels).

Index

Numbers in *italics* refer to page numbers on which illustrations appear.